PLANTING a Small Garden

RHS SIMPLE STEPS TO SUCCESS
PLANTING a Small Garden

Phil Clayton

SENIOR EDITOR Zia Allaway
SENIOR DESIGNERS Rachael Smith and Vanessa Hamilton
MANAGING EDITOR Anna Kruger
MANAGING ART EDITOR Alison Donovan
BOX AND COVERS DESIGN Nicola Powling,
Harriet Yeomans and Amy Keast
DTP DESIGNER Louise Waller
PICTURE RESEARCH Lucy Claxton,
Richard Dabb, Mel Watson
PRODUCTION CONTROLLER Rebecca Short

PRODUCED FOR DORLING KINDERSLEY
Airedale Publishing Limited
CREATIVE DIRECTOR Ruth Prentice
PRODUCTION MANAGER Amanda Jensen

PHOTOGRAPHY Mark Winwood

First published in Great Britain in 2007 by
Dorling Kindersley Ltd
Penguin Books Ltd
80 Strand
London WC2R 0RL
Reissued 2015

2 4 6 8 10 9 7 5 3 1

001–285150–Sept/2015

A CIP catalogue record for this book is available
from the British Library.

ISBN 978-0-2412-0687-4

Printed and bound in China.

To find out more about RHS membership, contact:
RHS Membership Department
PO Box 313, London SW1P 2PE
Telephone: 0845 130 4646
www.rhs.org.uk

Important notice
The author and the publishers can accept no liability for
any harm, damage, or illness arising from the use or
misuse of the plants described in this book.

A WORLD OF IDEAS:
SEE ALL THERE IS TO KNOW
www.dk.com

Contents

Designing with plants
Find inspiration in beautiful, imaginatively planted small gardens.

Where to start
Choose a planting style and discover more about your site and soil.

How to plant
Learn how to make and plant up flowerbeds and borders.

Planting recipes
Follow seasonal and themed planting combinations for different sites.

Container ideas
Select a beautiful container and plant it up using the seasonal recipes.

Looking after your garden
Discover how to keep your garden in peak condition throughout the year.

Plant guide
Use this guide to create beds and borders filled with colour, scent, and structure.

Index
Acknowledgements

Designing with plants

Planting a small garden can be challenging but it is also very rewarding. In this chapter, we look at some of the key factors that help to create successful planting schemes in small spaces. Try to disguise the boundaries, which will make the garden look larger. Focal points are important for leading the eye through the garden, while the style and colour schemes you choose help to shape the overall design. Think, too, about seasonal colour and form, and work in a selection of plants that provide interest at different times of the year.

Disguising boundaries

An exposed boundary, such as a fence or wall, can make a garden feel small and claustrophobic. Concealing boundaries with plants will radically improve the appearance of a garden, transforming it into an attractive space.

Pictures clockwise from top left
Back fence disguise In many gardens, the most obvious boundary is usually the back fence and, if visible, it immediately gives away the length of the garden. By creating a mixed border directly in front, using a range of plants that will grow as tall as, or taller than, the fence, you will succeed in blurring the edges of your plot. Make sure the border is a reasonable depth: a narrow strip in front of the fence, deep enough for only one plant, is likely to draw attention to the boundary rather than disguise it.

False perspective One of the most effective ways to disguise a boundary and also make a garden seem larger is by creating a false perspective. For example, in a garden that appears short, make the borders running down the sides of the garden taper outwards so that they are wider at their far end, making the garden appear longer. Another visual trick is to draw the eye away from the boundaries with a central, circular lawn or paved area, and surround it with dense planting. Evergreen shrubs will ensure that the effect lasts all year round.

Plant screen Dividing up the garden with various plant screens so that the entire garden is never completely visible from any one position will help make it feel larger and shift the emphasis away from the boundaries. Even a small plot can be divided up in this way using trellis or woven willow screens as supports for climbing plants; these also help to maximize growing space.

Courtyard enclosure Having a small garden does not mean that you should restrict yourself to small plants; in fact, doing so serves to underline a plot's limited size. Positioning a selection of quite large plants in front of fences or walls in generous-sized beds that have been pushed to the edges of the plot will help to maximize space in the centre of the garden, creating a courtyard. The plants will also help to hide fences and walls.

Using colour

The colour provided by flowers and foliage is particularly valuable in a garden. It can be used in a number of different ways, perhaps to evoke a particular mood or to give areas of the garden a theme or look.

Pictures clockwise from left

Rich colours If you spend a fair amount of time enjoying your garden from indoors, it makes sense to provide displays of rich colour that are easily visible from the house, perhaps in pots and containers on the terrace, or in beds and borders close to the windows. Harmonious colours that blend well together create a strong but restful feel; use softer, pastel hues further away from the house because they show up better at a distance than saturated colours.

Monochrome planting A garden or border composed of mostly white-flowering plants creates a cool, calming feel that is most striking at dusk, when the blooms glow in the fading light. Try using cream and pale yellow flowers, as well as very pale pink and blue ones, to prevent the effect from becoming stark and clinical. Silver-leaved and variegated plants will provide interest once the flowers have faded.

Hot hues Fiery colours, such as reds, oranges, and intense pinks, demand attention, but they should be used with care: they attract the eye away from softer shades and, if planted at the far end of the garden, may make the plot feel smaller. Often the simplest way to deal with hot-hued plants is to group them together and create a condensed and spectacular injection of colour. Alternatively, combine them with contrasting shades, such as rich blue or purple, to mitigate the effect.

Serene green It is important to remember that green is also a colour, and is the most commonplace in virtually every garden. There are many different shades of green but, generally, it has a restful effect, and gardens that are planted for foliage tend to be serene spaces. Set against other colours, though, green generally fades into the background, so use plants with variegated foliage or white or pastel-coloured flowers to shine out and provide additional interest.

Focal points

Gardens often benefit visually from a dramatic or arresting focal point, be it a statue, pot, or plant, which provides a point of reference within the design where the eye can rest.

Pictures clockwise from top left

Eye-catching trees In a garden that seeks to re-create the wild, focal points need to be natural objects, such as rocks or specimen plants. In this Mediterranean-style garden, the gnarled trunks and silvery foliage of a pair of old olive trees are as arresting as any classical sculpture.

Winding steps Even a utilitarian feature such as a flight of steps can provide a focal point, as long as it is well executed. Winding steps passing through lush foliage lead the eye on to brighter, more vibrant flowers and foliage, which then act as a visual full stop.

Dramatic containers Attractive pots and containers, planted or otherwise, are one of the simplest ways of creating a focal point. Used alone or in groups, they can be placed in a border, on a terrace, or at the end of a pathway, perhaps terminating a vista. Large, impressive pots are often best left empty; others can be enhanced with a dramatic plant, such as a *Dasylirion*.

Focus on colour Brightly coloured plants make small-scale focal points in beds and borders. The vivid flowers of bulbs, such as these orange tulips, provide short-term accents, lifting other planting and heightening interest.

Themed planting schemes

Some of the most successful gardens are developed around a particular theme or idea that helps to bind the planting and design together. Selecting plants that fit the overall concept help evoke the correct spirit and feel, which, in turn, lends a touch of authenticity to the garden.

Pictures clockwise from top left

Lush and subtropical There are many hardy and borderline hardy plants that can be used to create a subtropical-style garden. Generally, the lush feel is provided by foliage plants. Large specimens of hardy *Trachycarpus* palms, bamboos, phormiums, and tree ferns will provide structure; in summer, containers can be filled with tender plants such as begonias, cannas, *Lantana*, and gingers (*Hedychium*), which produce exotic flowers.

Classic Italian Italianate gardens tend to be rather formal, with plenty of topiary and clipped evergreens, such as box (*Buxus*). The layout is usually simple and the planting restrained, limited to a few favourites, such as acanthus, agapanthus, olives, slender conifers, jasmine, and herbs. Classical statuary plays an important role, often terminating a vista, and specimen plants in containers may feature, perhaps used along a terrace to introduce a sense of repetition and rhythm to the garden.

Meadow planting Informal and naturalistic, meadow planting uses a limited palette of different plants mixed randomly together in large groups. These schemes work well in large, open expanses and tend to be short-lived – many of the plants used are annuals, such as poppies (*Papaver*) and cornflowers (*Centaurea cyanus*). However, perennials can also feature, and the planting style scaled down to more modest-sized borders.

Moroccan oasis Water is a vital element for a Moroccan theme, and a wall fountain, perhaps with a blue-tiled surround, would make an ideal feature. Most of the planting should be in pots, with pelargoniums, date palms, agaves, and other succulents suitable choices, but avoid having too many plants. A few large foliage plants in darker corners, and climbers, such as *Trachelospermum*, scrambling up the walls would also fit in very well.

Themed planting schemes *continued*

Pictures clockwise from top left

Mediterranean style Gravel, terracotta pots, and a sunny site all help to create a Mediterranean feel. Avoid filling the garden with too much planting – the general scheme should not be too lush – and try a few formal elements, such as clipped box balls. Olive trees in pots can spend summer outside, while more permanent plants could include lavender (*Lavandula*), *Cistus*, and one or two exotics, such as *Yucca*.

Oriental calm Japanese-style gardens often feature a few manicured plants, such as Japanese maples (*Acer japonicum*), dwarf pines, bamboos, *Ophiopogon*, and *Ilex crenata,* set in a rock and gravel landscape. Strategically positioned bonsai specimens add a dramatic touch to the overall theme.

Cottage effects Borders overflowing with flowers are typical of cottage gardens. Old favourites include delphiniums, foxgloves (*Digitalis*), Shasta daisies (*Leucanthemum superbum*), and lavender (*Lavandula*), with sweetly-scented roses and self-seeding annuals completing the informal look.

Modern mixes Architectural plants, such as tree ferns, phormiums and *Tetrapanax*, are the mainstays of highly designed contemporary gardens. Grasses and small-scale, naturalistic planting schemes are also popular, their soft foliage forms contrasting well with hard modern landscaping materials, such as concrete, glass, and steel.

Seasonal interest

Watching the way a garden changes its character with the seasons is part of the joy of gardening. To get the most from your plot, it should be designed and planted to provide interest for every day of the year. Each season has its own distinctive feel and appearance, and a well-designed garden will include plants that reflect this.

Spring (*top right*) As the days lengthen, the garden quickly wakes from its winter rest. Bulbs, such as daffodils and crocuses, produce showy flowers, while other herbaceous plants begin to emerge from the ground, and deciduous shrubs and trees produce fresh, verdant growth.

Summer (*right*) For many gardeners, this season represents the high point of the year. Most herbaceous plants reach their zenith, filling out borders and blooming for several months, while annuals flower and set seed. Leafy trees and shrubs provide structure, and tender plants flourish in the mild summer months.

Autumn (*bottom right*) This is arguably the most colourful and plentiful season. Late-flowering plants, such as asters and dahlias, blaze in borders, while many trees and shrubs produce vivid berries and fruits. The leaves of many deciduous plants also brighten up the garden with rich hues before falling. In the moist and still warm conditions, some bulbs, such as *Colchicum*, provide a welcome freshness.

Winter (*opposite page*) Once all the leaves have fallen, the shape and structure of the garden and its plants can be properly appreciated. This is a season of quiet, subtle beauty. Trees and shrubs, such as silver birch (*Betula pendula*) and *Cornus* with its red-coloured stems, evergreen plants, as well as the faded seedheads of herbaceous plants, provide interest. A few plants also produce delicate, often sweetly scented flowers. As cold weather sets in, frost and snow dust the plants, creating a magical feel.

Spring beds and borders

No season is more eagerly anticipated than spring. After the dark, cold days of winter, the garden bursts into life with verdant growth and colourful flowers, marking the start of a new gardening year. In late spring many gardens look their freshest, resplendent with the soft, glowing greens of young foliage.

Pictures clockwise from left
Colourful climbers Walls and fences can be clothed with a range of different climbers that will flower in spring. Wisteria, grown for its waterfalls of scented purple or white flowers, is perhaps the most well known. It is, however, a large plant and needs restrictive pruning to keep it within bounds. Alternatives include *Clematis montana* in white or pink, and *Akebia quinata* with purple blooms, although these climbers are also potentially large. More suited to a small garden are *Clematis alpina, C. macropetala*, and the early honeysuckle *Lonicera periclymenum* 'Belgica' with its deliciously scented flowers.
Vibrant bulbs and early perennials In beds and borders, herbaceous plants push through the soil, growing quickly in the damp, mild conditions. Many will flower early, especially those that enjoy woodland conditions, such as *Pulmonaria, Primula, Dicentra, Doronicum, Epimedium,* and *Anemone.* Some of these perennials can be grown successfully with spring bulbs, such as tulips and daffodils, injecting extra interest into plantings and helping to mask yellowing bulb foliage as the season progresses.
Carpets of spring flowers In less formal areas of the garden, where a more naturalistic display is desired, it is possible to plant and even naturalize some bulbs in grass. Snowdrops (*Galanthus*) and crocuses that flower in early spring can be interplanted with fritillaries, tulips, daffodils (*Narcissus*), and *Camassia* to create a display that will last until early summer. Areas under mature trees are ideal for this kind of treatment, but avoid mowing the grass until the bulb foliage has died away.

Summer beds and borders

Summer is the season of unrestrained colour, when most beds and borders are at their best. If well planted, the garden should provide a succession of flowers that lasts for months on end.

Pictures clockwise from top left

Mixing colours Planting a mix of herbaceous perennials and annuals is a quick and easy way to provide striking contrasts. Colour-themed plantings that use a restricted colour palette are effective at creating different moods. Contrasting colours evoke drama, while those that blend together produce a more relaxed feel.

Continuous colour Many perennials run out of steam as the summer progresses, especially in times of drought or extreme heat. Others, though, can be relied on to flower well into autumn, especially those that are natives of warmer climates, such as *Crocosmia* and *Rudbeckia*.

Calming foliage Without some order, too many bright flowers can become rather overpowering, especially in a small space. The mitigating effect of foliage can help create a calmer effect, softening bright colours. Silvery leaves, such as those of *Artemisia*, used with whites, creams, and pale pinks produce a cool feel; deep green foliage contrasts well with brightly coloured flowers.

Summer bulbs Summer-flowering bulbs, such as lilies, gladioli, and *Galtonia*, are often overlooked but, planted directly into borders or put in pots and plunged into the ground, they pack a powerful punch of colour.

Autumn beds and borders

As the days shorten, colour and interest in the garden come from new sources: the leaves of some plants acquire fiery tints, and fruits and seedheads replace many flowers. Some blooms are at their best during autumn, too.

Pictures clockwise from left

Deciduous trees Trees and shrubs, such as Japanese maples (*Acer japonicum*) and *Rhus*, produce autumnal tints that provide a spectacular backdrop to other plantings. The coloured leaves remain eye-catching once they have fallen, especially around the flowers of late-blooming perennials and bulbs, such as *Cyclamen*.

Structural seedheads Some summer-flowering perennials, such as *Echinops*, *Allium*, *Agapanthus*, and many grasses, produce attractive seedheads that last well into winter. They look particularly striking in the sloping autumn light, decorated with cobwebs or, later, frost.

Colourful fruits Many shrubs and trees produce handsome, long-lasting fruits at this time of year; certain roses, in particular, carry ruby hips, as long as they are not pruned in autumn. Consider leaving other plants unpruned, such as *Viburnum* and *Sorbus*, to help provide birds with food.

Perennial colour Some perennials, such as *Aster*, *Chrysanthemum*, *Cyclamen*, and *Saxifraga fortunei*, will produce vibrant flowers until the first hard frosts, and look wonderful in autumnal borders. They can also be useful in containers to inject colour into areas of the garden that are of little interest at this time of the year.

Winter beds and borders

Gardens are often neglected in winter once most showy flowers have faded, but with the right plants they can still be enchanting places at this time of year. Plants with winter interest often have special, rather subtle qualities, such as sweetly scented flowers, attractive stems, foliage, seedheads, berries, or structural shapes.

Pictures clockwise from top left

Winter flowers Hellebores, such as *Helleborus* x *hybridus*, are among the best winter-blooming plants. Flowering from midwinter to mid-spring, these clump-forming evergreen perennials are easily grown in light shade in any good soil, and form good ground cover when planted in drifts. Other perennials with winter interest worth seeking out include mauve-flowered *Iris unguicularis* and *Arum italicum* 'Marmoratum', with its white-veined leaves.

Transient beauty Frost and snow add an element of short-lived beauty to the garden in winter, often transforming it overnight. A light covering of snow or a hard frost can enhance structures, highlighting architectural features and plants, and briefly changing the whole feel of a garden.

Scented highlights Mahonias are among the finest evergreen shrubs for winter, with their spiny foliage and sweetly scented yellow blooms, followed by blue-tinged berries. They are also useful for their architectural form, which makes them an attractive backdrop for other plants such as *Euonymus*, with its colourful fruit.

Graceful grasses The seedheads of some grasses will survive well into winter, providing a touch of unexpected grace to plantings, especially when dusted with frost. Translucent, they allow views through to plants behind, such as the fruit-laden branches of a crab apple (*Malus*).

Scented shrubs Some shrubs flower in winter, such as witch hazel (*Hamamelis*) with its orange, yellow, or red, spider-like blooms. Other shrubs worth considering for their delicious scent include the honeysuckle *Lonicera* x *purpusii* and *Chimonanthus praecox*.

Where to start

The most successful planting schemes are those that have been planned with care and forethought. When choosing a style, first think about the time you have to spend in the garden. Look through this chapter to discover which planting designs need regular weekly or even daily maintenance, and those that are easier to care for. The section on different designs provides inspiration and will help you to plan a garden to suit your needs and those of your household. When you have decided on the design, check your garden's site and soil to determine what plants will enjoy the conditions you can provide.

High and low maintenance

When planning a garden, be realistic about how much time you can afford to keep it looking at its best.

High maintenance

Gardens for plant lovers These gardens tend to be stocked with a wide range of choice plants, which will need their specific growing requirements matched in order to grow well. Careful placing of plants and constant manipulation of growing conditions by gardeners will keep these plots looking their best, and regular attention will be required to prevent plants outgrowing their space.

Dense planting Filling a garden with plants may reduce weeding, but competition for light and water causes problems. High-maintenance plants include tulips, which may need planting and lifting each year, annuals grown from seed, plants with specific watering, feeding, or pruning needs, and those prone to pests and diseases. A lawn also needs weekly mowing to keep it looking good.

High-maintenance planting suggestions

- *Aster* (some)
- *Astrantia*
- *Buxus* (if kept clipped)
- *Canna*
- *Clematis* (some)

- *Cornus sanguinea* 'Winter Beauty'
- *Dahlia*
- *Dicksonia antarctica*
- *Echinacea purpurea*

- *Erysimum*
- *Helenium*
- *Hosta*
- *Lavandula* (lavender)
- lilies

- *Melianthus major*
- roses (some)
- *Sambucus racemosa* 'Plumosa Aurea'
- tulips

Tulip bulbs should be planted in late autumn.

Hosta 'June', like all hostas, is loved by slugs.

Prune *Cornus sanguinea* in early spring.

Lilium regale bulbs should be planted in spring.

Low maintenance

Easy-care gardens These are a good choice for people with little spare time but who still want an attractive outdoor space. Lawns can be replaced by patios or decks, and the soil covered with a special membrane to cut down on weeding, and topped with bark or cobbles after planting. Irrigation systems can be installed, and plants chosen that do not need much attention.

Undemanding planting This can provide year-round interest and yet needs little attention. Large specimen plants provide immediate impact. Evergreen shrubs and trees are good because most need little pruning and do not drop leaves in autumn. Minimal use of herbaceous plants lessens end-of-season work, and using well-spaced larger plants reduces watering and trimming.

Low-maintenance planting suggestions

- *Acer*
- *Arbutus unedo*
- *Aucuba japonica*
- *Choisya ternata* Sundance
- *Cotoneaster horizontalis*

- *Fatsia japonica*
- *Hemerocallis* (day lily)
- *Ilex aquifolium* 'Silver Queen'
- *Jasminum nudiflorum*

- *Mahonia*
- *Nandina domestica*
- *Phormium*
- *Photinia* x *fraseri* 'Red Robin'

- *Phyllostachys nigra*
- *Stipa tenuissima*
- *Trachelospermum asiaticum*
- *Vinca* (periwinkle)

Ilex aquifolium 'Silver Queen' has beautiful evergreen foliage.

Stipa tenuissima is a trouble-free airy grass.

Hemerocallis 'Corky' is ablaze with golden blooms in summer.

Cotoneaster horizontalis has bright red autumn berries.

Choosing a planting style

When planting up your garden, if you decide to follow a particular style, first ensure that it is practical and fits your lifestyle.

What do you want?

Find inspiration for your plot by visiting other gardens, and looking at books, magazines, and television shows. If you long for a tropical garden with exotic plants, such as palms and other architectural specimens, you can achieve it with the use of containers on a sun-drenched terrace, even in the UK.

What do you need?

If entertaining outdoors is important to you, a large patio with a dining/barbecue area will be useful, while a lawn is a good idea if children are likely to play in the garden in summer. Your lifestyle may dictate that you have a low-maintenance garden with plants that are easy to care for, but look good all year round. Consider, also, how much privacy you need.

Examine the visual appeal of your chosen scheme. Will you include plants with impact to create impressive planting schemes? Or would you prefer a themed garden with an exotic feel, or simply an oasis of tranquillity. When selecting plants, make sure you choose those that will suit the style of garden you have in mind.

Keeping it neat

A wonderful garden filled with unusual plants and flowers is all very well, but it may require a great deal of time to keep it in tip-top condition. When planting and designing a garden, decide how much time you can spare to look after it. Some planting styles require less effort to keep them looking good than others. A formal garden with a central lawn, for example, looks tidy once mown, but it may be better to reduce the area of grass or replace it with gravel or decking, if free time is limited. Planting in formal schemes tends to be confined to geometric-shaped beds or borders. Designs can be either high-maintenance, with a mix of perennials, annuals, and shrubs, or low-maintenance, with easy-care shrub borders.

A natural approach

For many people, choosing a naturalistic planting style, using drifts of perennials or a large number of native plants, creates a garden that feels at one with nature. With this approach, you may also decide to avoid using chemicals on your plants, and adopt organic growing methods. Encourage birds, insects, and other wildlife into your garden, to enrich your gardening experience, and create curved or sinuous borders for your informal planting designs.

Planting style ideas

Setting a particular style for your planting and layout helps to create a feeling of cohesion, and makes selecting plants and garden objects much easier. The main hurdle is making a choice and sticking to it.

Oriental

An authentic Japanese garden is difficult to create, and requires discipline and subject knowledge. It is possible to use elements from the style, however, to create a distinctive oriental feel. Minimalist lines, the use of certain plants, rocks, raked gravel or slate chippings, and focal points, such as stone lanterns, prove effective. Colours are restrained, derived mostly from foliage; showy flowers are seldom used.

Planting suggestions
- *Acer japonicum* (Japanese maple)
- *Camellia sasanqua*
- *Ophiopogon* 'Nigrescens'
- *Phyllostachys nigra*
- *Pinus mugo* 'Ophir'

Maintenance tips Keep raked gravel weed- and leaf-free: the garden should appear immaculate.

Knot gardens and Parterres

Knot gardens are generally small scale and feature low, clipped hedges, usually box (*Buxus*) but sometimes *Santolina* or lavender (*Lavandula*), set out in simple patterns. Between the hedges are blocks of colour, normally from bedding plants or coloured gravel. Parterres are more ambitious in scale and design, but they also use low hedges with colourful flowers and often topiary. Both styles of garden are highly formal, labour intensive, and best seen from above.

Planting suggestions
- bedding plants, eg, dahlias, cosmos
- *Buxus sempervirens* (box)
- culinary herbs
- *Santolina chamaecyparissus*
- *Taxus baccata* (yew)

Maintenance tips Clip the hedges 2–3 times a year to keep them neat.

Modernist

The overall feel of most modernist gardens is one of simplicity and restraint, with planting often taking second place to hard landscaping, giving a minimalist feel. Plants are carefully selected and sited, with architectural specimen plants providing instant impact. The palette of plants is usually limited, with a restricted colour theme, and maximum use is made of form and texture. Broad sweeps of perennials and grasses, often planted in a naturalistic way, provide summer colour.

Planting suggestions
- *Acer japonicum* (Japanese maple)
- *Dicksonia antarctica*
- *Fatsia japonica*
- *Phyllostachys nigra*
- *Stipa tenuissima*
- topiary shapes, box (*Buxus*), yew (*Taxus*)
- *Verbena bonariensis*

Maintenance tips Modernist gardens tend to be naturally low maintenance, but ensure plants are well watered, especially when they are establishing, and top up mulches of gravel or aggregates, as required.

Maple foliage provides vibrant colour in an oriental-themed garden.

A well-tended knot garden makes a fine garden feature, even without flowers.

Clipped box balls in a sea of lavender give this garden a modern twist.

Tropical

For sheer floral drama, few gardening styles can match a tropical border. These displays of exotic-looking plants, usually a mix of hardy and tender plants grown for both foliage and flowers, provide great interest in both summer and autumn. Planting is informal, with plants massed together in profusion; huge bold leaves and vibrantly coloured flowers predominate, while the displays improve as the season progresses. This style is labour-intensive and displays usually last only until the first frosts.

Planting suggestions
- *Canna*
- dahlias
- *Hedychium gardnerianum*
- *Melianthus major*
- *Musa basjoo* (banana)
- *Phoenix canariensis*
- *Phormium tenax*
- *Ricinus communis*

Maintenance tips Plant out a tropical border after the last frosts have passed. Feed and water well for rapid, lush growth. Ensure you protect tender plants well from winter cold.

Cottage

A traditional cottage garden represents many people's idea of the ultimate garden. Planting tends to be informal, but contained within a simple, formal layout, which is usually little more than a network of paths. Flowering herbaceous perennials predominate, and these gardens are usually at their best in early summer. Later on, roses and clematis provide plenty of colour, and in winter, well-chosen shrubs lend the garden structure once the flowers have faded. Colours are often soft and muted, giving a relaxed feel.

Planting suggestions
- *Astrantia*
- delphiniums
- *Dianthus* (pinks)
- *Digitalis purpurea* (foxglove)
- geraniums
- *Philadelphus*
- *Ribes* (flowering currant)
- roses

Maintenance tips Regular top-ups of garden compost in spring will keep perennials growing well. Remember to divide clumps of herbaceous plants every 2–3 years for healthy growth.

Contemporary

The contemporary garden is usually thought of as an extension of the home, a so-called "outdoor room" that often includes dining and seating areas. This modern and practical garden style often features expanses of hard standing or wooden decking, ideal for massed displays of brightly coloured yet colour-themed container plants in the summer. Beds tend to be filled with easy-care, usually evergreen plants, to provide year-round interest, and are often planted through a weed-suppressing membrane, topped with mulch to minimize aftercare.

Planting suggestions
- *Acer japonicum* (Japanese maple)
- *Astelia nervosa*
- *Aucuba japonica* (spotted laurel)
- *Photinia* 'Red Robin'
- *Choisya ternata*
- *Clematis armandii*
- *Pittosporum tenuifolium* 'Tom Thumb'

Maintenance tips Ensure plants are well watered while establishing. Keep mulches topped up, and plant containers when frost has passed.

Spectacular flowers and foliage provide high-impact summer displays.

Borders overflowing with flowers are typical of the cottage-garden style.

Wooden decking is used to give this garden a contemporary feel.

The effects of aspect

The direction in which your garden faces affects the amount of sunlight it receives, while altitude influences temperatures. Take both factors into account when choosing your plants.

Which way does your garden face? Simply observing how much sun your garden receives gives an idea of its orientation. To work it out accurately, use a compass. Stand with your back to your house wall – the reading from here shows the direction your garden faces. South-facing gardens get the most sun; north-facing sites the least.

Morning: areas that are in sun now may be in shade by the afternoon.

Sunny and shady sites Some gardens are sunnier than others as a result of their aspect and other factors, such as shade-casting buildings, but in all sites, the amount of direct sun and the sun's position in the garden change as the day progresses. A south-facing garden will have sun all day; north-facing much less, perhaps none in winter.

Sunny gardens are usually more desirable, but shade does have its advantages. These gardens are cooler, have a more humid microclimate, and are less prone to drought. There are many wonderful shade-loving plants that will not tolerate direct sun, while in a sunny garden, slightly tender plants from Mediterranean regions, for example, flourish. The key is to work with what you have.

Midday: the sun is overhead, so the garden receives maximum sunlight.   Evening: as the sun sets, the glancing light casts soft shadows.

Beware frost pockets Frost occurs when temperatures fall below freezing. Spring frosts can be particularly lethal in the garden, especially where many near-tender plants are grown. Even on a local scale, some sites will be more vulnerable than others, usually in areas where pockets of freezing air develop. Cold air is heavy, and sinks to the lowest point. If it cannot escape, it collects, forming a "frost pocket". Here, frosts will be harder and linger longer, and you may get a frost when other areas remain above freezing. Gardens in valleys or in a hollow often suffer badly. Hedges or walls may create or worsen the effect, preventing cold air from flowing down the hillside. Thinning a hedge, using trellis instead of a solid barrier, or leaving a gate open on cold nights may help.

Creating microclimates Even within a single garden, you may notice great differences in the growing conditions. A border by a sunny wall or fence will be far warmer and drier than one in the shade, perhaps beneath a tree, which is likely to be more humid with a more even temperature range. A low-lying area will remain wetter than a border at the top of a slope, and some parts of the garden may be sheltered, others exposed. Gardeners can capitalize on these differences; even in small areas, they allow you to grow a wider range of plants. A sunny spot can be enhanced with a raised bed to improve drainage for tender plants; low-lying areas could be turned into a bog garden for moisture-loving plants. You can make a windy area more sheltered with a permeable barrier, such as a trellis.

Seasonal impact The direction your garden faces gives it particular properties throughout the year. A north-facing garden, or border in front of a north-facing fence, will receive little sun in winter, remaining cold and damp, but temperatures will be more constant than in a south-facing area that is warmed after a sunny winter day, only to be chilled at night. Plants exposed to constant chill also start into growth later, but are affected less by late frosts. While potentially dank in winter, a north-facing area offers a cool retreat in summer, and lush, moisture-loving woodland plants will thrive there. Spring bulbs take advantage of the sun spots under bare deciduous trees, areas that receive little light in summer. Sunny patios are ideal for tender plants, but may get too hot and dry in summer for some plants.

Understanding soils

Before you decide what to plant in your garden, take a look at the soil. The acidity or alkalinity of the soil and its composition determine what will grow, and an understanding of its properties helps you to keep plants in good health.

Types of soil

Soils comprise two elements: a mineral portion (tiny particles of weathered rock, larger gravels, and stones) and an organic (dead plant and animal remains, and living organisms). The most important part of the soil is found in the top 30cm (12in). Below this lies less fertile subsoil.

Soil particle size, the amount of organic matter, and available water determine soil characteristics. The smallest soil particles will form clay, those a little larger create silts, and even bigger particles form sandy soils. Soils with a mix of different particle sizes are known as loams.

The descriptions below will help determine your soil type:

Chalk soil Soils that are pale and contain chunks of white limestone (usually the underlying rock) and often flint, are chalk soils. They are free-draining and fertile, often rather thin, and almost always alkaline.

Peat soil Distinctively dark, peat soils are rich in organic matter that helps them retain soil moisture. Peat forms where wet, acid conditions stop plant and animal remains decomposing fully. These soils are usually acidic.

Clay soil Composed of more than 25 per cent moisture-retaining clay particles, clay is heavy to dig and may be waterlogged in winter (it dries out in summer). Organic matter is easily trapped, resulting in good fertility.

Silty soil With particles not as fine as those of a clay soil, silts are also fairly moisture-retentive and fertile. They tend to be dark in colour, which is the result of the accumulated organic matter that they often contain.

Sandy soil Sandy soils are easy to spot, being light and free-draining. They are composed of relatively large individual soil particles that allow water to drain quickly.

Testing the soil's acidity or alkalinity

Use a soil-testing kit to assess the acidity or alkalinity (pH) of your soil – the results will indicate what plants will grow well. Carry out several tests across the garden, using soil from just below the surface. Soil pH is measured on a scale of 1–14. Above neutral (7) is alkaline, below is acidic; pH 6.5 is usually considered the optimum.

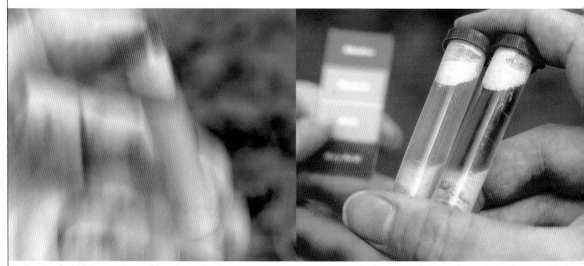

Following the kit's instructions, add garden soil and water to the test tube provided and shake the contents well.

Compare results from around the garden with the chart provided: a red/yellow colour shows an acid soil; dark green an alkaline one.

Testing sandy soil

To determine whether your garden has a sandy soil, and thus one that may need regular irrigation and boosting with organic matter, carry out a simple test to examine the texture of the soil. Take your sample from just below the soil surface and repeat at intervals across the garden to ensure an even overall result.

Rub a small amount of soil between your fingers. If the soil has a gritty, granular feel, it is likely to contain a high proportion of sand.

Try to squeeze the soil into a ball – the grains of a sandy soil will not stick together but if it is loamy, the shape may hold a little.

Testing clay soil

To check if you have clay soil, and thus one that may become waterlogged in winter and be more difficult to dig than other soil types, remove small samples of soil from different spots around the garden from just below the soil surface. Clay soil will feel quite sticky and heavy when shaped in the hand.

Try to mould the soil in your hands – the particles of a clay soil will hold together well and change shape when pressed.

Heavy clay can even be rolled into a thin cylinder; it will often appear smooth and shiny.

Making the most of your soil

Different types of soil have differing characteristics, some aiding cultivation of certain plants, others providing a challenge to gardeners. Various techniques can be used to improve the soil to maximize its potential.

Sandy soil

Advantages Sandy soil is free-draining, which prevents plants from becoming waterlogged in winter and aids the survival of species sensitive to wet conditions. It is easy and light to dig all year round, and warms up quickly in the spring.

Disadvantages In dry conditions, plants will often require extra irrigation, and moisture-loving species will be unreliable in these soils. Sandy soils have a tendency to be poor, so you will need to apply plenty of plant food and organic matter.

Improving sandy soil Dig in large amounts of organic matter each year to help improve the soil's ability to hold water and nutrients. Mulches such as gravel help to keep in moisture. Digging in clay may also be useful.

Plants for sandy soils

- *Acacia dealbata*
- *Calluna vulgaris* 'Silver Knight'
- *Catananche caerulea*
- *Cistus* x *hybridus*
- *Convolvulus cneorum*
- *Cotoneaster horizontalis*
- *Erysimum* 'Bowles' Mauve'
- *Euphorbia characias*
- *Euphorbia rigida*
- *Grevillea* 'Canberra Gem'
- *Helianthemum* 'Rhodanthe Carneum' ('Wisley Pink')
- *Helleborus argutifolius*
- *Iris unguicularis*
- *Melianthus major*
- *Olea europaea* (olive)
- *Pittosporum tobira*
- *Romneya coulteri*
- *Rosmarinus officinalis* (rosemary)
- *Solanum crispum* 'Glasnevin'
- *Verbena bonariensis*

Abutilon x suntense

Allium hollandicum 'Purple Sensation'

Artemisia alba 'Canescens'

Bupleurum fruticosum

Lavandula stoechas

Perovskia 'Blue Spire'

Clay soil

Advantages Clay soils are usually highly fertile and many plants thrive in them. They also retain water well. The more clay soil is worked, the better it is for planting, as the soil gradually becomes more crumbly and drainage improves. Avoid working the soil when it is wet and easily compacted.

Disadvantages Despite its high fertility, a clay soil has a number of problems that can be hard to tackle. In winter it may become waterlogged and impossible to dig. Attempts to work the soil in this state usually create compaction where the soil particles are compressed, resulting in yet further waterlogging. In summer, the opposite problem occurs; clay bakes hard and even simple digging can be impossible. Even when soils are manageable they are heavy, breaking into large clods, and they are slow to warm up in spring.

Improving clay soil The key to success is often simply perseverance. By adding organic matter to the soil, you will eventually improve its structure, making it more crumbly and easier to work. In small areas, perhaps in a raised bed, dig in horticultural grit. Avoid walking on the garden when it is waterlogged and do not dig the soil when wet. Try to carry out most planting in spring or autumn when the soil is more manageable. In areas where waterlogging is severe, you may need to install drains.

Plants for clay soils

- *Alchemilla mollis*
- *Arum italicum* subsp. *italicum* 'Marmoratum'
- *Aruncus dioicus*
- *Aucuba japonica* (spotted laurel)
- *Berberis darwinii*
- *Buxus sempervirens* (box)

- *Campanula glomerata*
- *Carex elata*
- *Cornus sanguinea* 'Winter Beauty'
- *Digitalis purpurea* (foxglove)
- *Geranium*
- *Hemerocallis* (day lily)
- *Hosta*

- *Hydrangea macrophylla* 'Lanarth White'
- *Iris laevigata*
- *Jasminum nudiflorum*
- *Leycesteria formosa*
- *Mahonia* x *media* 'Buckland'
- *Viburnum tinus* 'Eve Price'

Anemone x *hybrida* 'Honorine Jobert'   *Euphorbia characias*   *Iris sibirica* 'Perry's Blue'

Malus 'John Downie'   *Primula pulverulenta*   *Sambucus racemosa* 'Plumosa Aurea'

Making the most of your soil *continued*

Alkaline soil

Advantages An alkaline soil enables you to grow a wide range of plants; many vegetables (such as members of the cabbage family) will not grow as well in acidic soil. Ornamentals, such as clematis, are said to grow better in an alkaline soil, and the finest rose gardens tend to be in alkaline areas. These soils suit earthworms; some pests and diseases, such as club root, are less of a problem.

Disadvantages There are certain plants that simply will not grow in alkaline conditions and, unfortunately they are often among the most desirable. Rhododendrons, camellias, *Pieris*, some magnolias, and other woodland plants, such as *Uvularia* and *Trillium*, need the cool, moist, acid soil associated with their native habitats. These plants are known as "calcifuge" or lime-hating. Some acid-loving plants may survive on alkaline soils but will look sick, with yellowing leaves (chlorosis). Alkaline soils tend to be deficient in manganese, boron, and phosphorus, all of which are important for healthy plant growth.

Improving alkaline soil You cannot, as such, improve alkaline soil, since a high pH can be both good and bad. Gardeners are best advised to grow what suits their particular soil. Many acid-loving plants can be grown in containers, or in a raised bed filled with ericaceous (acid) compost. Where the soil pH is neutral or just alkaline, years of adding organic matter may lower the pH enough for some smaller acid-loving plants.

Plants for alkaline soils

- *Aquilegia* McKana Group
- *Aster* 'Coombe Fishacre'
- *Buddleja davidii* 'Dartmoor'
- *Buxus sempervirens*
- *Choisya ternata* Sundance
- *Clematis*
- *Cotoneaster horizontalis*
- *Erica carnea* 'Foxhollow'
- *Erysimum* 'Bowles Mauve'
- *Hebe*
- *Hibiscus syriacus* 'Oiseau Bleu'
- *Iris unguicularis*
- *Lavandula stoechas*
- *Mahonia* x *media* 'Buckland'
- *Nepeta* x *faassenii*
- *Phormium* 'Yellow Wave'
- *Primula vulgaris*
- *Pulsatilla vulgaris*
- roses
- *Salvia officinalis* 'Purpurascens'
- *Sedum* 'Herbstfreude'

Alchemilla mollis   *Campanula glomerata*   *Clematis cirrhosa*

Cotinus coggygria 'Royal Purple'   *Jasminum nudiflorum*   *Lonicera* (honeysuckle)

Acid soil

Advantages Some of the most spectacular garden plants, including rhododendrons, *Meconopsis*, and *Desfontainia*, will grow well only on acidic soil. Other species, such as *Hamamelis*, may survive on alkaline soil but simply perform better on acid. Few garden plants will not tolerate a mildly acid soil, although a very low pH will limit your choice. Acid soils are often associated with woodland conditions and tend to be cool and moist.

Disadvantages Acid soil, though usually rich in organic matter, can be quite poor, especially if it is also sandy. To improve it, dig in plenty of well-rotted manure each year. Very peaty soils can, conversely, be waterlogged and require draining. These are often the most acid of

all and you may need to add lime to them for a range of plants to thrive. Most fruit and veg do not like strongly acid soil and other plants simply will not grow – these are known as "calcicoles" or lime-loving. Acid soils are often deficient in phosphorus and may have too much manganese and aluminium for healthy plant growth.

Improving acid soils If your soil is strongly acidic, you may need to increase the pH to broaden the range of plants you can grow. Adding spent mushroom compost is an excellent way of doing this. Powdered lime is an alternative. However, most gardeners usually feel that a mildly acidic soil is desirable, and simply grow plants that enjoy their conditions.

Plants for acid soils

- *Astilboides tabularis*
- *Betula* (birch)
- *Camellia*
- *Cercis canadensis* 'Forest Pansy'
- *Cornus canadensis*
- *Corydalis flexuosa*
- *Daphne bholua* 'Jacqueline Postill'

- *Desfontainea spinosa*
- *Digitalis purpurea* (foxglove)
- *Hedychium densiflorum*
- *Leucothoe fontanesiana* 'Rainbow'
- *Meconopsis*
- *Photinia* x *fraseri* 'Red Robin'

- *Pieris*
- *Primula pulverulenta*
- *Rhododendron*
- *Romneya coulteri*
- *Skimmia* x *confusa* 'Kew Green'
- *Stewartia monadelpha*
- *Uvularia grandiflora*

Acer palmatum   *Calluna vulgaris* 'Silver Knight'   *Carex elata* 'Aurea'

Cornus kousa var. *chinensis*   *Grevillea* 'Canberra Gem'   *Hydrangea quercifolia*

How to plant

In this chapter, discover how to make a border from scratch, removing grass and weeds, and feeding and improving the soil before planting. To complete your border, choose from the selection of edging and mulches, and find out how to make garden compost to encourage strong, healthy plant growth. Also, learn how to plant up your beds and borders with trees, shrubs, climbers, perennials, and annuals to create colourful displays throughout the year.

Making a border

Flower and shrub borders provide colour, scent, and seasonal interest, making them an essential part of the garden. Follow these basic steps when planning and preparing your borders to ensure their success through the year.

1 Decide where in the garden you want your border and mark out its shape. For a curved edge, use a garden hose. Make sure the border is not too narrow and that its shape fits well within the overall layout of the garden.

2 Using a half-moon turf cutter or a small spade, carefully slice through the grass, following the contours of the hose. Make sure the cuts join up properly and push the full depth of the cutter into the ground.

3 With a spade, begin stripping off the turf. Cut it into manageable-sized squares from above, then slide the blade of the spade under the roots of the grass. Try to avoid removing an excessively deep layer of soil.

4 Stack the turves in a spare corner of the garden, grass-side down. The soil in these turves is nutrient-rich and should be reused. After several months, the grass will die off and the pile can be cut up, sieved, and dug into the borders.

Making a border *continued*

5 Dig over the exposed soil with a fork, pushing the tines down to their full depth. Remove old roots, large stones, and debris that you unearth, and break up large clods of soil. Work the soil until it has a crumbly texture.

6 With a spade, spread about 5cm (2in) of organic matter, such as well-rotted farmyard manure or garden compost, over the surface of the border. Turn the compost into the soil, and mix it in evenly.

7 If the soil is heavy or poorly drained, spread an 8cm (3in) layer of coarse grit or gravel over it, and dig this into the top 15cm (6in) of soil with a spade. This will help open up drainage channels through the soil in the root zone.

8 Using a soil rake, remove any remaining stones, roots, or debris that may have worked their way up to the surface. Then, with the flat back of the rake, carefully level off any mounds and hollows.

VERBENA
rigida

Tip for success

To stop soil spilling out onto the lawn, consider adding edging to the front of the border before planting. Use a spirit level to make sure the edging is level.

9 Set out the plants, still in their pots, on the ground, adjusting their positions until you are happy. Pay attention to their eventual size, flower and foliage colour, and season of interest to achieve your desired effect.

Finishing touches

To help set off planting and add a touch of "polish" to the garden, small additions, such as edgings and mulches, can make a big impact.

Soft lawn edging

It is surprising how much difference a well-edged lawn makes to the overall look of a garden. Where borders meet grass, trim with edging shears after mowing to maintain the shape of the lawn. Edging irons are also useful for reshaping when required. Plants that spill from borders onto the lawn may add a touch of informality, but will damage the lawn in the long run.

Choosing a hard edge

Borders that meet with hard landscaping materials require less maintenance than soft edging. Sprawling plants are best grown next to hard surfaces where the border's shape can be maintained more easily. Use paving for formal or informal situations, and areas where grass struggles to grow, such as in shade or next to narrow paths.

Brick edging Laid as a path or in a single row between a border and lawn, or along gravel paths, bricks create a traditional feel. They also blend well with planting.

Paved edging Where paving meets a border, attractive informal effects can be achieved. Allow plants, such as lavender, to billow out from flower beds, softening the hard layout.

Wood edging If you have border soil to retain, wood edging is an easy-to-install option. Partially conceal with planting to help it blend in, and apply wood preservative to prevent rotting.

The benefits of mulching

Mulches help to conserve soil moisture, reduce weeding, provide a decorative element, and some add organic matter to soil, improving its fertility and promoting plant growth. A mulch is simply a layer of material spread over the soil surface, and different situations and planting require different types. Avoid applying them too thickly – about 3cm (1¼in) is ideal – or over the crowns of plants. Mulches are usually applied in early spring.

Organic matter Garden compost or well-rotted manure is an ideal mulch because it aids plant growth, improves the soil and helps retain moisture. It needs re-applying every year.

Cocoa shells Lightweight and easy to apply, cocoa shells break down, enriching the soil. They are, however, easily disturbed by wind, animals, or birds, and can look unsightly.

Gravel Long-lasting and inexpensive, gravel preserves moisture in summer and keeps damp away from sensitive plants, such as alpines, in the winter. It is heavy to apply.

Decorative mulches Coloured glass chippings, crushed seashells, and other decorative mulches are ideal for pots and containers. They will reduce weeds and conserve moisture.

Weed membranes Laid beneath mulches before planting, porous membranes drastically reduce weeds. Adding plants after a membrane has been laid can be tricky, though.

Bark chips Lightweight, organic, and weed-suppressing, bark chips are a popular mulch, but as they slowly break down, they may remove valuable nitrogen from the soil.

Making your own compost

Making compost from your kitchen and garden waste is a sustainable and environmentally friendly way of recycling. Applied as a mulch, compost helps to improve the fertility and moisture-retaining qualities of your soil.

Types of composter The basic way of making compost is to pile it into a heap, but this can be unsightly, and better compost is often achieved more quickly using a composter. The simplest structures are bays, usually made of corrugated plastic or metal, in which waste is piled. Wooden compost bins are easier on the eye, and can be built at home from scrap wood; otherwise you can buy ready-made bins, often with slatted sides or vents for air circulation. Effective and inexpensive, lightweight plastic compost bins (*right*) are also a popular choice.

Filling your bin Almost any vegetable matter can be added to a compost bin and the more diverse the range of materials, the better the compost. It is also important to keep woody and nitrogen-rich leafy materials in proportion: you should try to include about twice as much woody material (twigs, paper) as nitrogen rich-material (grass, kitchen scraps). Mix grass cuttings with woodier clippings or even shredded paper, because a thick layer of grass will inhibit important air movement. Chop bigger cuttings into small pieces and avoid adding weeds with seeds, or persistent perennial weeds. Place a layer of coarser twigs in the bottom of the bin and then add the material in layers. Spread a little farmyard manure between layers to help speed up the composting process.

Leafy material adds nitrogen and moisture:
• Grass clippings and weeds
• Kitchen vegetable waste
• Fallen leaves
• Herbaceous plant clippings
• Sappy hedge trimmings
• Windfall fruit
• Old bedding plant material

Woody, carbon-rich material improves airflow:
• Woody plant clippings and twigs
• Shredded paper
• Scraps of cardboard
• Untreated wood shavings
• Stems of herbaceous plants
• Bark mulch

Layer woody and leafy material in your compost heap.

Speeding up composting Nitrogen-rich manure contains micro-organisms that promote composting, so add it to your heap to help the material break down more quickly. Alternatively, you can buy special compost additives. Turning the heap also improves air circulation, speeds up rotting, and ensures that all the material is composted.

Tip for success

Too much wet, green, nitrogen-rich material, such as grass clippings, will quickly turn the compost heap sour and smelly. Mix it with coarser woody matter in layers, and aim to turn the heap regularly.

Planting a perennial

Perennials are plants that grow from year to year, and many are long-lived. But for these plants to perform well as they mature, they must be planted and established with care.

1 Place the plant in its pot on the ground in a position that suits its growing needs and not too close to other plants. The soil in the pot should be thoroughly soaked before planting to help give the plant a good start.

2 With a spade, dig a hole wider and deeper than the size of the plant's container. Add organic matter, such as garden compost, to the base of the hole and dig it in well. Pour some water into the hole before planting.

3 Remove the plant carefully from its pot. If the roots tightly encircle the root ball, the plant is pot-bound and the roots need to be teased out gently. Place the plant in the hole, slightly deeper in the ground than when it was in its pot.

4 Backfill in around the root ball, firming the soil as you go and ensuring the plant stands straight in its hole. Avoid mounding the soil around the stems; the plant should be in the centre of a shallow depression. Water well.

Planting a tree

Planting a tree may seem a simple task, but these plants are long-lived and should be planted well and given the appropriate aftercare if they are to fulfil their potential in years to come.

1 Soak the root ball of the tree in its container before planting. This will compensate for any water loss from the roots during the planting process and ensure that the tree settles into its position well.

2 With a spade, dig a planting hole about three times as wide as the diameter of the pot and 30cm (12in) deep (most root activity takes place in the top layer of soil). Lightly fork the base and sides of the hole.

3 Check the hole is the correct depth by putting the pot in the hole and placing a cane across the top – it should rest on both sides of the hole and on the top of the root ball. You may need to add or remove soil in the hole.

4 Gently remove the root ball from its pot – the pot should slide off easily, leaving the root ball intact. Carefully tease out some of the larger encircling roots, to help the tree root into the surrounding ground more successfully.

Planting a tree *continued*

5 Stand the tree in its final position. Drive a stout stake into the ground close to the tree trunk and at a 45° angle over the root ball, to avoid damaging the roots. Make sure that the stake faces into the prevailing wind.

6 Backfill the hole with soil, working it in around the roots. Unless the soil is poor or sandy, do not add organic matter because this seems to prevent the roots spreading out in search of nutrients. Firm the soil in gently.

7 Tie the tree quite loosely to the stake with a tree tie, about 45cm (18in) from the ground, to allow the stem to flex in the wind. Check the tie regularly and loosen it as the tree girth expands, to prevent damage to the bark.

8 Water the tree well after planting and during dry periods for the first couple of seasons. Add a mulch of well-rotted garden compost, about 8cm (3in) deep, around the tree. Keep the mulch about 15cm (6in) away from the trunk.

9 Over the next two to three years, use sharp secateurs to remove any damaged wood or branches that spoil the tree's shape, such as crossing, rubbing branches. Do not leave stumps, cutting fairly close to the main stem.

Planting a shrub

Shrubs form the backbone of a planting scheme, providing important structure as well as flower and foliage effects. Before planting, check the plant label for the shrub's preferred site and soil, since moving it at a later date will be difficult.

Tip for success

Once planted, apply a top-dressing of fertilizer above the roots in spring. Later watering or rain will wash it down.

1 Soak the plant thoroughly in its pot. With a spade, dig a large hole, approximately two to three times the diameter of the pot. Remove any old roots and large stones, and break up the soil in the base of the hole with a fork.

2 To check the hole is the correct depth, place a cane across the top; it should rest on both sides of the hole and on the top of the root ball. Position the plant with its best side facing the direction from which it will be viewed.

3 Remove the pot; it should slide off easily, leaving the root ball intact. Tease out any encircling roots. Add organic matter, such as garden compost, to the removed soil, especially if it is poor. Backfill around the root ball.

4 Firm the earth down gently. The plant should sit at the centre of a shallow depression, which will assist watering. Spread a mulch of organic matter around the plant, keeping it away from the stems. Water the plant well.

Planting a climber

Climbing plants are particularly useful in small gardens because they add height without too much bulk, maximizing the use of limited space. They are also a quick and effective way of covering dull fences and garden structures.

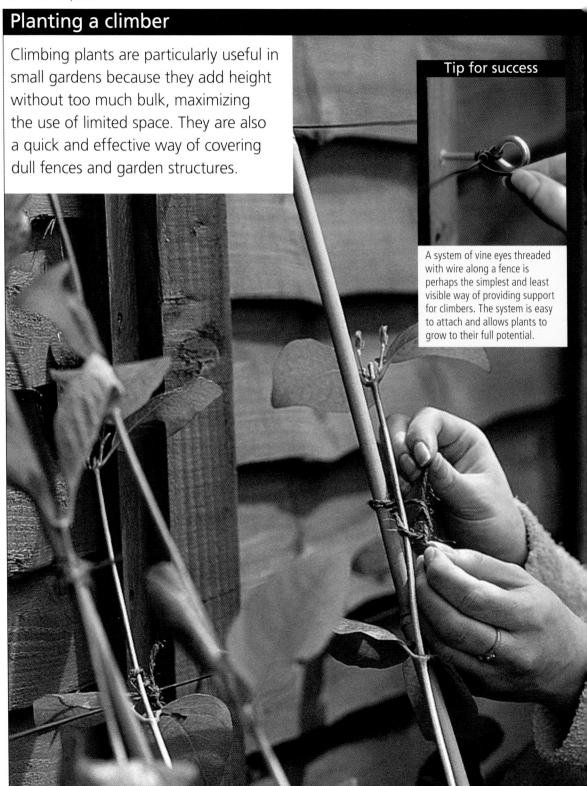

Tip for success

A system of vine eyes threaded with wire along a fence is perhaps the simplest and least visible way of providing support for climbers. The system is easy to attach and allows plants to grow to their full potential.

1 Dig a hole twice the diameter of the root ball, 30–40cm (12–16in) from the fence. To support the stems and achieve good initial coverage, construct a fan from canes pushed into the soil and angled towards the fence.

2 Make sure the plant is well watered, then position it in the hole at an angle pointing towards the fence. Carefully remove the pot and any supporting stakes. Separate multiple stems growing from the base of the plant.

3 Backfill the hole with the removed soil mixed with some organic matter, such as garden compost. Firm the soil gently as you go. The plant should be at the centre of a shallow depression, to aid watering and establishment.

4 Select the stems to be trained up the canes, tying in one to two stems per cane with gardener's twine. Spread a mulch of bark chips or organic matter over the soil to keep in the moisture and suppress weeds.

Sowing annuals outside

Many hardy annuals, such as California poppies (*Eschscholzia*), are best sown *in situ* outside, avoiding the root disturbance that occurs when seedlings are removed from their pots. Plants grow quickly to give fine summer displays.

Tip for success

The fine soil of a seedbed is attractive to cats, and young seedlings may be disturbed by birds. To avoid these problems, protect the area with twiggy sticks pushed into the ground.

1 Select an open area without any competing plants for sowing the seeds. Lightly fork over the soil, breaking up large clods, and then remove large stones, weeds, and debris with a rake. Work the soil into a fine, level tilth.

2 Make drills (shallow depressions to sow seed into) in the soil by pushing a pole or bamboo cane into the soil surface. Drills make it easier to identify seedlings; weed seedlings are unlikely to emerge in straight lines.

3 Place the seeds into the palm of your hand, and aim to pour the seed gently from a crease as you pass your hand along the drill. Do not sow the seed too thickly. Larger seeds can be placed in the drill with your fingertips.

4 Lightly cover the drills with fine soil and water well using a can with a fine rose to avoid disturbing the seeds. Keep the seedbed moist and remove any weeds. When the seedlings emerge, carefully thin out close-growing plants.

Sowing hardy annuals

While many hardy annuals can be sown outside *in situ*, it is often safer and more rewarding to plant seeds in pots under cover, either in a cold frame, greenhouse, or on a sunny windowsill.

Tip for success

Always label your seeds using a waterproof pen. Include the name of the plant and the date of sowing.

1 Fill a clean or new 9cm (3½in) pot with a good-quality seed-sowing compost, leaving a 2–3cm (¾–1¼in) gap beneath the rim of the pot. Firm the compost gently to create an even surface for the seeds.

2 Using a watering can with a fine rose spray, dampen the compost, being careful not to disturb it by splashing too much. Alternatively, stand the pots in a tray of water until the surface is moist, then remove.

3 Sow the seed evenly. Large seeds are easy to position, but fine seeds should be spread from the palm of the hand. Some seeds need to be covered by a fine layer of compost or vermiculite; follow the instructions on the seed packet.

4 When the seeds have germinated and produced a few sets of leaves, harden them off by placing the pots outside during the day for a few weeks. Then you can plant them out in the garden.

Planting recipes

The recipes in this chapter illustrate a range of exciting planting combinations for all seasons, helping you to create beautiful beds and borders. The symbols below are used in the recipes to show the conditions preferred by each plant.

Key to plant symbols

♀ Plants given the RHS Award of Garden Merit

Soil preference

○ Well-drained soil

◐ Moist soil

● Wet soil

Preference for sun or shade

☼ Full sun

☼ Partial or dappled shade

☀ Full shade

Hardiness ratings

❋❋❋ Fully hardy plants

❋❋ Plants that survive outside in mild regions or sheltered sites

❋ Plants that need protection from frost over winter

❦ Tender plants that do not tolerate any degree of frost

Sun-baked gravel garden

In a sunny corner, a gravel garden offers the chance to grow an interesting range of plants: herbs with aromatic leaves, plants with silvery foliage, alpines, and some grasses are good choices. These plants enjoy growing through gravel because it keeps excessive moisture away from their stems, yet helps to keep the roots cool and moist. Gravel also warms up quickly during the day and retains warmth at night.

Border basics

Size 3x2m (10x6ft)

Suits Herbs, low-growing plants, annuals, bulbs, grey-leaved plants

Soil Well-drained, poor soils

Site Open and sunny, not too exposed

Shopping list

- 2 x *Parahebe perfoliata*
- 1 x *Helictotrichon sempervirens*
- 1 x *Thymus pulegioides* 'Bertram Anderson'
- 1 x *Santolina chamaecyparissus*
- 1 x *Aurinia saxatilis* 'Variegata'
- 1 x *Rosmarinus officinalis* Prostratus Group

Planting and aftercare

Dig over the site, removing large stones, rubbish, and weeds; spot-treat perennial weeds like bindweed, because they will be hard to remove once gravel is spread. Add organic matter, such as well-rotted garden compost, to the soil, and dig in plenty of gravel to at least a spade's depth to help provide good drainage.

Place any feature rocks or driftwood as focal points. Position plants with plenty of space between each one. Add grit to the planting holes and place plants slightly proud of the soil surface. As you spread the gravel, work some into the crowns of plants. Water well. Once settled, the plants will need watering only in the driest periods.

Parahebe perfoliata
❀❀ ◌ ☀ ♛

Helictotrichon sempervirens
❀❀❀ ◌ ☀ ♛

Thymus pulegioides 'Bertram Anderson' ❀❀❀ ◌ ☀ ♛

Santolina chamaecyparissus
❀❀ ◌ ☀ ♛

Aurinia saxatilis 'Variegata'
❀❀❀ ◌ ☀

Rosmarinus officinalis Prostratus Group ❀❀ ◌ ☀

Cottage garden medley

This ever-popular, typically English style of planting uses mainly herbaceous flowering plants in a relaxed, informal way. The flowers are usually pale pastel colours with a few brighter hues added as highlights. Traditional cottage garden favourites include delphiniums, foxgloves (*Digitalis*), verbascums, penstemons, as well as woody plants, such as roses and lavender (*Lavandula*). Although not low maintenance, such planting schemes are certainly beautiful in summer, when the plants all bloom together in profusion.

Border basics

Size 2x1.5m (6x5ft)

Suits A mixture of herbaceous perennials

Soil Well drained

Site Sunny with some shelter from wind

Shopping list

- 3 x *Delphinium grandiflorum* 'Summer Blues'
- 3 x *Verbascum* x *hybridum* 'Snow Maiden'
- 3 x *Delphinium* 'New Zealand Hybrids'
- 3 x *Geum* 'Blazing Sunset'
- 3 x *Penstemon digitalis* 'Husker Red'
- 3 x *Digitalis purpurea*

Planting and aftercare

Prepare the border before planting, adding well-rotted farmyard manure. Ensure drainage is good; if not, add some gravel. Planting in spring is best for perennials. Three of each plant will guarantee a decent show of flowers in the first year, and odd numbers of plants look best in informal plantings. Plant in small drifts, with taller plants positioned towards the back, but do not be too rigid about this – the effect should appear relaxed. The delphiniums, in particular, may need staking with canes or pea-sticks. In autumn after flowering or the following spring, cut down old foliage, and mulch with manure.

Delphinium grandiflorum 'Summer Blues' ✿✿✿ ◐ ☼

Verbascum x *hybridum* 'Snow Maiden' ✿✿✿ ◌ ☼

Delphinium New Zealand Hybrids ✿✿✿ ◐ ☼

Geum 'Blazing Sunset' ✿✿✿ ◐ ◌ ☼

Penstemon digitalis 'Husker Red' ✿✿ ◐ ◌ ☼

Foliage effects

Raised beds are easy to maintain and can be constructed almost anywhere. For a contemporary look, planting should be colourful and stylish, and provide year-round interest. Pick plants that complement each other in a range of colours and textures – here, much of the interest is provided by foliage.

Bed basics

Size 1x1m (3x3ft)

Suits A range of non-vigorous plants with similar requirements

Soil Moist but well drained

Site Sunny, and sheltered from strong, drying winds

Shopping list

- 1 x *Euphorbia amygdaloides* 'Purpurea'
- 1 x *Sedum spectabile*
- 1 x *Carex comans* 'Frosted Curls' or *Molinia caerulea* subsp. *caerulea* 'Variegata'
- 3 x *Ophiopogon planiscapus* 'Nigrescens'
- 1 x *Heuchera* 'Plum Pudding'

Planting and aftercare

Any raised bed must have adequate drainage holes; without them the plants will rot. A layer of crocks or polystyrene at the base will help water to run away freely. In a small bed, use a soil-based compost mixed with some organic matter, such as well-rotted manure; a large bed should be filled with good-quality topsoil with some well-rotted garden compost worked into it. Leave the bed for a few days to let the soil settle. Position shorter plants, such as the *Ophiopogon*, at the edges, and taller plants, like the *Euphorbia*, in the centre of the bed. Water well. Make sure that the compost never dries out, weed the bed regularly, and cut down any faded herbaceous growth, such as the *Sedum* flowerheads, in autumn or spring.

Euphorbia amygdaloides 'Purpurea'
❋❋❋ ◗ ☼

Sedum spectabile
❋❋❋ ◊ ☼ ♛

Carex comans 'Frosted Curls'
❋❋ ◗ ◊ ☼

Ophiopogon planiscapus 'Nigrescens'
❋❋❋ ◗ ◊ ☼ ♛

Heuchera 'Plum Pudding'
❋❋❋ ◗ ◊ ☼

Alternative plant idea

Molinia caerulea subsp. *caerulea* 'Variegata' ❋❋❋ ◗ ◊ ☼ ♛

Tree and shrub combination

Trees and shrubs can be used to create exciting combinations for beds and borders. They also tend to require less maintenance than herbaceous plants, and retain structure and sometimes foliage over winter. Include a range of growth habits and sizes, foliage colour and texture, plants with attractive flowers and others with winter interest, all of which will thrive in the given conditions.

Border basics

Size 3x2.5m (10x8ft)

Suits Wide range of shrubs and small trees; compact selections are best

Soil Acidic, free-draining, moisture-retentive soil

Site Sunny and sheltered

Shopping list

- 1 x *Aucuba japonica* 'Picturata'
- 1 x *Cotinus* 'Grace'
- 1 x *Phormium tenax* 'Atropurpureum'
- 1 x *Grevillea juniperina*
- 1 x *Magnolia grandiflora* 'Goliath'
- 1 x *Pittosporum tobira* 'Nanum'

Planting and aftercare

Dig the soil thoroughly, adding plenty of rotted garden compost. Space plants out well because they will be difficult to move when larger. The biggest plant is likely to be the magnolia, so put it at the back of the border. The evergreen gold-splashed foliage of the *Aucuba* is a focal point, so position the plant centrally. Its rounded form contrasts well with the spiky *Phormium*. The lower-growing *Pittosporum* and *Grevillea* (which needs acid soil) can be placed at the front. The *Cotinus* balances the composition, its purple leaves matching those of the *Phormium*. Make sure all are well watered and firmed in at planting. Some pruning, especially of the *Grevillea* and *Cotinus*, may be required later on, to stop them outgrowing their positions.

Aucuba japonica 'Picturata'
❄❄❄ ◗ ◊ ☼

Cotinus 'Grace'
❄❄❄ ◗ ◊ ☼

Phormium tenax 'Atropurpureum'
❄❄ ◗ ◊ ☼

Grevillea juniperina
❄❄ ◊ ☼

Magnolia grandiflora 'Goliath'
❄❄❄ ◗ ◊ ☼

Pittosporum tobira 'Nanum'
❄❄ ◊ ☼

Spring hot spot

Vibrant, fiery colours are not solely for late summer; there are various perennials and bulbs that provide similar hues in late spring, although the effect is different. The reds, oranges, and yellows of plants such as tulips, the first lupins, *Doronicum*, and *Euphorbia* can be combined with verdant new growth to create a glowing display.

These hot colour combinations contrast with the whites, blues, and cool yellows found in abundance elsewhere at this time, making a dazzling display.

Border basics

Size   2x2m (6x6ft)
Suits   Early-flowering perennials, bulbs (especially tulips), perennials with attractive young foliage
Soil   Any fertile and moist soil
Site   Sheltered with some direct sun

Shopping list

- 20 x *Tulipa* 'Ballerina'
- 20 x tulips of contrasting shape
- 5 x *Polygonatum* x *hybridum*
- 5 x *Euphorbia griffithii* 'Fireglow'
- 5 x *Foeniculum vulgare* 'Purpureum' (just visible)

Planting and aftercare

Prepare the border by adding plenty of organic matter, such as garden compost, to the soil. Position the perennials first, with the tallest plant, Solomon's seal (*Polygonatum*), towards the back. Interplant the *Euphorbia* with the bronze fennel (*Foeniculum*), leaving reasonable spaces in between to allow planting pockets for the tulips. Plant the bulbs at three times their depth, in eight groups of five. Avoid mixing the tulip cultivars because this will dilute the effect.

The *Euphorbia*, in particular, will suffer if the soil becomes too dry. Watch out for sawfly larvae on the Solomon's seal.

Tulipa 'Ballerina'
❋❋❋ ◐ ◇ ☼ ♼

Polygonatum x *hybridum*
❋❋❋ ◐ ☼ ♼

Tulipa (pinky-red)
❋❋❋ ◐ ◇ ☼

Euphorbia griffithii 'Fireglow'
❋❋❋ ◐ ☼

Lush leaves for shade

In a shaded courtyard or corner of a terrace, a modern planting scheme in a raised bed can create a dramatic, rather exotic, effect. Many foliage plants grow well in some shade, and a mix of evergreen shrubs and herbaceous plants provides year-round interest. A tall bamboo (*Phyllostachys*) will catch the breeze, adding a dynamic element to the planting, while a few variegated plants, such as hostas, help lift the planting out of the shadows, as will painting the backdrop and raised walls a pale colour.

Border basics

Size 2.5x1.5m (8x5ft)

Suits Lush foliage plants

Soil Fertile and moisture-retentive

Site Sheltered, semi-shaded corner

Shopping list

- 2 x *Hosta* 'Francee'
- 1 x *Hebe salicifolia*
- 3 x *Fatsia japonica*
- 1 x *Phyllostachys nigra*
- 1 x *Miscanthus sinensis* 'Variegatus'
- 3 x *Ophiopogon planiscapus* 'Nigrescens'
- 2 x *Hedera helix* (ivies)

Planting and aftercare

Make sure the bed has enough drainage holes to prevent waterlogging. Choose a good quality topsoil and add well-rotted manure to it before planting. Position taller plants at the back (the bamboo will look best in the corner). The hostas, *Ophiopogon*, and ivies should go at the front. Contrast the hand-shaped foliage of the *Fatsia* with the white-edged blades of the *Miscanthus*. Spread white or grey pebbles as a mulch over the soil, and water the plants in well, ensuring they do not go short of water while establishing. Aftercare is easy: cut down old herbaceous growth in late autumn or spring, and watch out for slugs.

Hosta 'Francee'
❄❄❄ ◐ ◊ ☼ ▵ ♔

Hebe salicifolia
❄❄ ◐ ◊ ☼

Fatsia japonica
❄❄ ◐ ◊ ◊ ☼ ◑ ♔

Phyllostachys nigra
❄❄❄ ◐ ◊ ◊ ☼ ◑ ♔

Miscanthus sinensis 'Variegatus'
❄❄❄ ◐ ◊ ☼ ♔

Ophiopogon planiscapus 'Nigrescens'
❄❄❄ ◐ ◊ ☼ ◑ ♔

Formal front garden

Small front gardens lend themselves to formal planting. Traditionally, these designs feature a low perimeter wall of clipped box (*Buxus*) hedges in a simple shape, such as a square, filled with a mixture of brightly coloured foliage and flowering plants, some tender, others perennials. There is often a central "dot plant," such as a *Cordyline*, to serve as a focal point. Any bare soil is then mulched with a layer of gravel. This helps to reduce weeding and keeps the garden looking smart.

Pelargonium (red)
❀ ◐ ○ ☼

Deschampsia flexuosa 'Tatra Gold'
❋❋❋ ◐ ☼

Border basics

Size 1.5x1.5m (5x5 ft)

Suits Box hedges, bright tender perennials, colourful hardy plants

Soil Ideally, fertile, well drained, and not too dry

Site Small, formal situation, preferably with some sun

Shopping list

- 5 x *Pelargonium* (red)
- 3 x *Deschampsia flexuosa* 'Tatra Gold'
- 2 x *Phormium* 'Tom Thumb'
- 1 x *Penstemon digitalis* 'Husker Red'
- *Buxus sempervirens* (enough to make a border)
- 3 x *Spiraea japonica* 'White Gold'

Phormium 'Tom Thumb'
❋❋ ◐ ○ ☼

Penstemon digitalis 'Husker Red'
❋❋ ◐ ○ ☼

Planting and aftercare

Dig over the site, removing any weeds, and add well-rotted organic matter, such as manure. Firm and level the soil with a rake. Plant the box plants first, about 15–20 cm (6–8 in) apart, to form the framework of your design. Then arrange the remaining plants in bands of colour. The border will need regular upkeep to keep it looking immaculate. Deadhead the pelargonium throughout the season; in early summer, trim the box and, if required, the spiraea. In spring, replace the tender pelargoniums and reduce the flowering stems of the penstemons.

Buxus sempervirens
❋❋❋ ◐ ○ ☼ ◑

Spiraea japonica 'White Gold'
❋❋❋ ◐ ○ ☼

Mediterranean moods

Choose the sunniest spot in the garden, away from cold winds, and select plants reminiscent of Mediterranean holidays: irises, grasses, euphorbias, and evergreen shrubs, such as olearia. Add herbs, like rosemary or sage, and bright-flowered bulbs, such as alliums. Terracotta pots planted with more tender species, such as succulent agaves, will help reinforce the Mediterranean feel.

Border basics

Size 3x3m (10x10ft)

Suits Grasses, neat evergreen shrubs, irises, bulbs, herbs, succulents, semi-tender plants

Soil Any free-draining

Site Sunny and sheltered, ideally by a wall

Shopping list

- 3 x *Iris* 'Jane Phillips'
- 1 x *Olearia x haastii*
- 3 x *Euphorbia characias* subsp. *wulfenii*
- 5 x *Allium hollandicum* 'Purple Sensation'
- 1 x *Anemanthele lessoniana* (*Stipa arundinacea*)
- 1 x *Bergenia cordifolia*
- 2 x *Ballota pseudodictamnus*

Planting and aftercare

Dig over the soil, removing any stones and weeds, and add plenty of organic matter, such as manure. If the site is not well drained, dig in gravel. Set taller plants at the back of the border, at least 30cm (12in) from the base of the wall. Plant shrubs and perennials first; bulbs are best planted in drifts around the key plants later. The iris rhizomes should be near the soil surface, so that they are partially exposed. Mulch with gravel and water well.

Remove the flowering stems of irises after the blooms have faded. In spring, cut out the previous year's flowering stems of euphorbias as close to the base as possible, avoiding the toxic sap.

Iris 'Jane Phillips'

Olearia x haastii

bia characias subsp. *wulfenii*
◊ ☼ ♔

Allium hollandicum 'Purple
Sensation' ❋❋❋ ◊ ☼ ♔

Anemanthele lessoniana
❋❋ ◊ ☼

Mixed herb tapestry

Well-planted herb borders should delight the senses: not only are they attractive to look at, but the aroma of foliage and flowers provides an extra element of interest, and some herbs can also be used to flavour food. Many have variegated or silver leaves, so they are still attractive when out of flower. Try also to include some evergreen herbs, such as lavender (*Lavandula*) or rosemary (*Rosmarinus*).

Border basics

Size 2x2m (6x6ft)

Suits Culinary herbs, such as thyme, oregano, marjoram, sage, chives, rosemary, and also those with more medicinal properties, such as lavender and feverfew

Soil Any well-drained, fairly poor soil

Site An open site in sun, but not too exposed to cold

Shopping list

- 10 x *Origanum vulgare* 'Polyphant'
- 5 x *Lavandula angustifolia* 'Twickel Purple' or *Salvia officinalis* 'Icterina'
- 10 x *Thymus doerfleri* 'Doone Valley'
- 10 x *Thymus* x *citriodorus*
- 10 x *Origanum vulgare* 'Aureum'

Planting and aftercare

Try adopting a formal pattern with the plants, as in the style of a simple knot garden. The plants can be positioned in rows or bands, where they will knit together well. The lavender is the tallest plant and should go at the back, or in the centre if the bed is circular; the variegated sage *Salvia officinalis* 'Icterina' could be used as a culinary alternative. Next, plant contrasting bands of the smaller herbs.

A gravel mulch placed over the soil after planting helps to suppress weeds and keeps winter wet away from the crowns of the plants.

Origanum vulgare 'Polyphant'
✿✿✿ ◊ ☼

Lavandula angustifolia 'Twickel Purple' ✿✿✿ ◊ ☼

Thymus doerfleri 'Doone Valley'
✿✿✿ ◊ ☼

Thymus x *citriodorus*
✿✿✿ ◊ ☼

Origanum vulgare 'Aureum'
✿✿✿ ◊ ☼ ♈

Alternative plant idea

Salvia officinalis 'Icterina'
✿✿ ◊ ☼ ♈

Autumn elegance

A border designed for a fine autumn scheme can make a great addition to the garden. After the dazzling displays of summer, this is a forgotten season in many gardens, and yet there are many plants that are at their best at this time. Certain grasses and various other late performing perennials, such as *Sedum*, *Aster*, *Salvia*, *Kniphofia*, and *Verbena*, can be combined with the seedheads of plants that flowered in summer, perhaps set against the vivid autumnal hues of deciduous shrubs and trees.

Border basics

Size 3x3m (10x10ft)

Suits Late-flowering perennials, grasses, and plants with ornamental seedheads or berries

Soil Any well-drained, fertile soil

Site An open site in sun, not too exposed

Shopping list

- 3 x *Stipa gigantea*
- 7 x *Verbena bonariensis*
- 7 x *Sedum* 'Herbstfreude'
- 5 x *Calamagrostis brachytricha*
- 3 x *Perovskia* 'Blue Spire'

Planting and aftercare

For this scheme, it is better to plant in sweeps rather than groups for a more flowing effect. The *Stipa* is the tallest plant, so place towards the back. In front, plant the dainty *Perovskia* and upright *Calamagrostis*. This grass flowers earlier in the season, but in autumn the seedheads are an attractive rich brown. Allow the grass to mingle with the *Sedum*, best planted towards the front in a broad sweep, providing contrast and intense colour. Dot the slender *Verbena* throughout because its transparent form provides no visual barrier.

Retain the seedheads of these plants for as long as possible, cutting down in spring before new growth begins.

Stipa gigantea
✿✿✿ ◊◊ ☼ ♛

Verbena bonariensis
✿✿ ◊ ☼ ♛

Sedum 'Herbstfreude'
✿✿✿ ◊ ☼ ♛

Calamagrostis brachytricha
✿✿✿ ◊◊ ☼

Winter blaze

Although winter is the season of snow and ice, there is still plenty to see in the garden if you include plants that provide seemingly unseasonal colour. The stems of some deciduous shrubs, such as *Cornus* and *Salix*, are brightly hued, and the foliage of many conifers intensifies in colour as low temperatures bite. A few plants produce showy flowers during this season, in particular winter heathers (*Erica*), but also bulbs such as snowdrops (*Galanthus*) and winter aconites (*Aconitum*).

Border basics

Size 3x3m (10x10ft)

Suits A range of winter interest plants

Soil Reasonably well drained and not too dry

Site Somewhere open that catches the winter sun

Shopping list

- 1 x *Chamaecyparis lawsoniana* 'Elwoodii'
- 9 x *Erica* x *darleyensis* 'Archie Graham'
- 5 x *Cornus sanguinea* 'Winter Beauty'
- 1 x *Pinus sylvestris* Aurea Group
- 7 x white *Erica carnea*

Planting and aftercare

Position the *Chamaecyparis* towards the back of the border – it will serve as a fine foil for the brighter colours. The golden pine (*Pinus*) should also be towards the back, in front of the *Chamaecyparis*. Plant the *Cornus* in a drift, mostly in the middle of the border, edging towards the front. Underplant with the heathers, creating seams of colour. Do not intermingle the colours.

The best stem colour from the *Cornus* is found on young growth, so after a couple of years, cut out one-third of old stems from each plant annually in spring. Trim the winter heathers with shears after they have flowered.

Chamaecyparis lawsoniana 'Elwoodii' ❄❄❄ ◐ ◌ ☼ ♔

Erica x *darleyensis* 'Archie Graham' ❄❄❄ ◐ ◌ ☼

Cornus sanguinea 'Winter Beauty' ❄❄❄ ◐ ☼

Pinus sylvestris Aurea Group ❄❄❄ ◐ ◌ ☼ ♔

Container ideas

Plants in pots and containers are great assets in a small garden. Inject colour into a deck or patio with pots filled with seasonal bedding, and plant up a backdrop of containerized shrubs to create a permanent framework. Pots can also be used to stop gaps in lack-lustre beds and borders, or to brighten up walls and windowsills. In this chapter, you will find tips on choosing the best containers for your garden, and how to look after them, as well as a few seasonal recipes to follow. (*See p.69 for key to plant symbols.*)

Choosing a container

When selecting pots and containers from the wide range available at garden centres, there are some key factors to take into account before you buy. As well as choosing a style, shape, and colour that suits your garden design, also consider the material from which the container is made, since each has its pros and cons.

Clay pots

Clay pots may be glazed or unglazed, coloured or patterned, light or dark in colour. Orange terracotta brings a taste of the Mediterranean to the garden.

Advantages They are attractive to look at, and can make a long-lasting addition to the garden, often improving with age and wear. There is a clay pot for most situations, and they can represent good value for money.

Disadvantages Many clay pots are not fully frost-proof and are prone to winter damage. They are also best avoided in exposed sites because they are easily broken. Fired clay is a porous material, so plants can dry out quickly, especially in summer, and moving these containers can be hard work since they are often heavy.

Metal containers

Containers made of metal may seem like a contemporary idea, but in fact some of the most desirable antique pots are lead, and suitable for a range of situations. Modern metal containers tend to be made of steel or galvanized aluminium and are simply styled, unlike lead planters, which feature more elaborate, classical designs.

Advantages By nature, metal containers are long-lasting, and can be heavy (especially lead ones), which makes them good for open sites. They can also be very stylish.

Disadvantages Metal containers can be expensive, particularly those made of lead; these are also exceptionally heavy. They also usually look out of place in an informal garden and may not suit some plants.

Wooden containers

Wood is a good material for a planter; it is soft and easily shaped, weathers well if treated with preservative, and suits a range of situations. It is also hard wearing and can tolerate rough treatment.

Advantages Although fairly lightweight and therefore easily moved, wooden containers are strong and durable. They are also most attractive and a good choice for situations where large planters are required.

Disadvantages Good-quality wooden containers can be quite expensive, especially those suited to more formal sites. They also need regular treatment with preservative to keep them looking good. Ensure they are made from sustainably harvested timber.

Stone containers

Pots and containers made of stone make beautiful ornamental planters. Granite containers can be used to give a Japanese feel, while old stone sinks suit alpines and other small plants.

Advantages Stone containers are very heavy, so not easily stolen or blown over, and long-lasting. Stone also looks good and gives a feel of permanency, especially once it has become colonized with mosses and lichens.

Disadvantages Genuine stone containers are very expensive, antique ones especially so, and you may feel that a concrete alternative is better value. The weight of stone must also be considered when transporting the pot and manoeuvring it into place in the garden.

Synthetic pots

Plastic has long been used as a material for pots and it may be disguised to look like clay, wood, or stone, although not always very convincingly. Increasingly, resins and other new materials are being used instead of plastic.

Advantages Synthetic pots are generally lightweight and easy to handle and transport. They tend to be tougher and more durable (and frost-resistant) than clay, and are far cheaper than stone or lead alternatives.

Disadvantages Synthetic pots lack the charm of traditional materials: an authentic stone, lead, or even clay planter feels more characterful than one made of plastic. Synthetic pots do not age well and may have a short life span. Being light, they are easily blown over.

Plant up a colourful container

One of the simplest ways of injecting seasonal interest into your garden is to plant up a few pots. Follow these easy guidelines to help ensure that your displays are attractive and long-lasting.

1 Before you plant the container, add water-retaining crystals to the compost. These swell up once moist, and provide plants with an extra reservoir of water, which helps to ensure plants do not suffer during dry spells.

2 Arrange your selected plants in their original pots in the container to see how they look – this way, adjustments can be easily made. When you are satisfied, remove the plants from their pots and plant up the container.

3 Fill around the plants with compost when they are in their final positions, and ensure you leave a 5cm (2in) gap between the top of the soil and the rim of the container, to allow for easy watering and a gravel mulch.

4 Spread a 2cm (¾in) deep gravel mulch over the top of the compost to help to conserve moisture in summer, deter weeds, and prevent unsightly compost splash when watering. It also makes an attractive finish to the planting.

Spring selection

Few plants are a more welcome sight than spring-flowering bulbs, and most are easy to grow and care for. These versatile plants are wonderful for pots and windowboxes or for planting out in the garden, and they can be treated as permanent planting or simply discarded after flowering. A good selection should provide colour over a long period, from the first snowdrops in late winter to the last tulips in early summer. Try planting the same types of bulbs together in pots and grouping them, or mix them.

Container basics

Size Approx. 15cm (6in) diameter terracotta pots

Suits Potted flowering bulbs

Soil Free-draining

Site Sunny, not too exposed

Shopping list

- 6 x *Hyacinthus orientalis* 'Ostara'
- 12 x *Narcissus* 'Sweetness'
- 10 x *Iris winogradowii*
- 12 x *Iris reticulata*
- 6 x *Iris* 'Katharine Hodgkin' or *Muscari armeniacum*

Planting and aftercare

Many spring bulbs are bought as bare dry bulbs in autumn, before they have come into active growth. It is important to choose firm, healthy bulbs and to plant them as soon as possible. Observe the correct planting depth for each kind of bulb, using free-draining multi-purpose compost with plenty of crocks in the base of each pot. Keep the pots somewhere sheltered. As the bulbs begin to grow, water more freely.

Once the flowers have faded, either discard the bulbs or allow the foliage to yellow and wither. Bulbs may then be lifted, dried, and replanted in pots, or put in the garden in autumn.

Hyacinthus orientalis 'Ostara'
✿✿✿ ◐◊ ☼ ♔

Narcissus 'Sweetness'
✿✿✿ ◐◊ ☼ ♔

Iris winogradowii
✿✿✿ ◐◊ ☼ ♔

Iris reticulata
✿✿✿ ◐◊ ☼ ♔

Iris 'Katharine Hodgkin'
✿✿✿ ◐◊ ☼ ♔

Alternative plant idea

Muscari armeniacum
✿✿✿ ◐◊ ☼ ♔

Sizzling tropics

A themed planting of subtropical species in a large pot will look dramatic and exotic until the first frosts. Choose a mix of bold foliage and flowers, and try to use a limited palette of "hot colours" to tie in with the terracotta pot. Arrange the larger plants towards the centre and back. The scheme will look most effective against a neutral background, where the textures and colours of the plants can be more easily appreciated.

Container basics

Size Approx. 60x60cm (24x24in) square terracotta pot or a similar-sized round one

Suits Subtropical plants with bold flowers and foliage

Compost Good-quality, multi-purpose

Site A sheltered, sunny position

Shopping list

- 1 x *Canna* 'Musifolia'
- 3 x *Begonia fuchsioides*
- 3 x *Crocosmia* x *crocosmiiflora* 'Star of the East'
- 1 x *Pelargonium tomentosum*
- 1 x *Isoplexis canariensis*
- 2 x *Canna* (orange hybrid)

Planting and aftercare

Arrange the plants carefully in their pots before planting them to see how they will look in their final positions. The scented foliage of the pelargonium is best used spilling over the pot's edge. Place plenty of crocks in the base of the container before pouring in the compost. After planting, water well and keep in a glasshouse or cool, light area indoors before placing the pot outside once any danger of frost has passed. Feed the plants regularly during the summer and make sure the compost is kept moist. Deadhead the canna as the blooms fade to encourage further flowers. In autumn, before the first frosts, bring the pot under cover.

Canna 'Musifolia'
❄ ◐ ◊ ☼ ♉

Begonia fuchsioides
❄ ◐ ☼ ♉

Crocosmia x *crocosmiiflora* 'Star of the East' ❄ ❄ ◐ ☼ ♉

Pelargonium tomentosum
❄ ◊ ☼ ♉

Isoplexis canariensis
❄ ◊ ☼

Canna (orange hybrid)
❄ ◐ ◊ ☼

Colour clash

For a dramatic and eye-catching container display, well-considered colour clashes can produce the best results, although the careful use of texture and form is even more important in such schemes. Here, yellow variegated foliage contrasts harmoniously with the dark glazed pot, while the rich red mini petunias (*Calibrachoa*) clash. Touches of red in the linear foliage of the grass *Hakonechloa*, though, help to tie the planting together. The gently arching growth of the grass is complemented by the trailing periwinkle (*Vinca*), which mingles well with the petunias that spill over the sides of the pot.

Container basics

Size Approx. 40cm (16in) diameter glazed pot

Suits A mix of bedding plants and garden perennials

Compost Good-quality, multi-purpose

Site A sheltered, sunny position

Shopping list

- 2 x *Hakonechloa macra* 'Aureola'
- 4 x *Calibrachoa* Million Bells Cherry
- 4 x *Calibrachoa* Million Bells Red
- 4 x *Vinca minor* 'Illumination'

Planting and aftercare

Place a good layer of crocks in the base of the pot for drainage, and add the compost. Position the grass centrally and then plant the *Vinca* and mini petunias around the outside. The petunias are frost-tender but they will flower for a long season in a sunny position, provided they are kept well fed and watered. In a more shaded spot, the petunias can be substituted by a red busy Lizzie (*Impatiens*) or a bedding begonia. After the frosts have browned the bedding, surviving plants can be planted out in the garden, or kept in the pot and used again the following year.

Hakonechloa macra 'Aureola'
❀❀❀❀ ◊ ☼ ☼ ☼ ☀ ♧

Calibrachoa Million Bells Cherry
❀ ◊ ☼

Calibrachoa Million Bells Red
❀ ◊ ☼

Vinca minor 'Illumination'
❀❀❀ ◊ ◊ ☼ ☼ ☀

Fire and ice

A striking combination of silvery-blue foliage and flame-red flowers gives this autumn interest container great appeal. The flower-power is provided by bedding cyclamen, which often prove surprisingly hardy in a sheltered situation, and should flower well from autumn until the first really hard frosts. White crocuses could continue the show in spring. Bright silver *Senecio*, tufts of the blue grass *Festuca glauca*, and an upright juniper complete the display. A matching pair of these planted pots would look particularly striking on either side of a doorway.

Container basics

Size Approx. 40cm (16in) diameter terracotta pot

Suits Evergreens and winter bedding plants

Compost Good-quality multi-purpose

Site A sheltered spot in semi-shade

Shopping list

- 1 x *Juniperus chinensis* 'Stricta'
- 2 x *Festuca glauca* 'Elijah Blue'
- 5 x *Senecio cineraria*
- 3 x *Cyclamen hederifolium*

Planting and aftercare

Place a layer of crocks in the pot and three-quarters fill with compost. Plant the juniper centrally towards the back of the pot and use the grasses to help soften the edges. The cyclamen and *Senecio* can be mingled at the front. (If you are including crocuses, plant them now; they will appear in spring, replacing any cyclamen killed by sustained hard frost.) Top up the pot with compost, water well, and place in a sheltered spot in good light. Keep the compost moist but not wet, and deadhead the cyclamen flowers as they fade to prolong the display. In late spring, the hardy plants can be planted out in the garden, or transferred to a larger container.

Juniperus chinensis 'Stricta'

Senecio cineraria

Cyclamen hederifolium

Festuca glauca 'Elijah Blue'

Winter perfume

This attractive display provides colourful winter cheer and a delicious spicy scent, which comes from the *Sarcococca confusa*, a neat evergreen shrub with little white blooms. While not particularly showy, they scent the air for several weeks. Flower and foliage colour is provided by winter pansies (*Viola*), a variegated standard *Euonymus*, and ivy (*Hedera*) to soften the rim of the barrel. You could also add primroses (*Primula vulgaris*), which flower into spring.

Container basics

Size Approx. 60cm (24in) diameter wooden half-barrel

Suits Winter bedding and evergreen shrubs

Compost Multi-purpose with added John Innes compost

Site A sunny, sheltered spot by a doorway

Shopping list

- 5 x *Hedera helix* 'Glacier'
- 5 x yellow winter pansies
- 5 x pale yellow winter pansies or 3 x double yellow primroses
- 3 x *Sarcococca confusa*
- 1 x *Euonymus fortunei* Blondy (standard-trained)

Planting and aftercare

Place crocks at the bottom of the barrel and three-quarters fill with compost. Arrange the plants with the *Euonymus* in the middle, underplanted with the *Sarcococca*, the ivies over the edges of the barrel, and the pansies and primroses in between. Fill in around the plants with compost. Water well and keep moist. Position the container where the perfume of the *Sarcococca* will be enjoyed. Remove faded blooms as the season progresses, and any plain green shoots on the *Euonymus*. In summer, replace the bedding with summer flowers, such as busy Lizzies or begonias.

Hedera helix 'Glacier'
❁❁❁ ◗ ◗ ☼ ♈

Yellow winter pansies
❁❁❁ ◗ ◗ ☼

Pale yellow winter pansies
❁❁❁ ◗ ◗ ☼

Sarcococca confusa
❁❁❁ ◗ ◗ ☼ ☼ ♈

Euonymus fortunei Blondy
❁❁❁ ◗ ◗ ☼ ☼ ♈

Alternative plant idea

Primula vulgaris 'Double Sulphur'
❁❁❁ ◗ ☼

Looking after your garden

Shrubs, trees, and herbaceous plants that receive a good supply of water and nutrients will reward you year after year with lush leaves and plentiful flowers and berries. In this chapter, discover the best ways to water without wastage, and how to provide just the right amount of food for your plants. Keeping beds and borders free of weeds, pests, and diseases is another challenge, but by following the advice given here on how to tackle these plant problems you can help to minimize the effects of all three.

Wise ways to water

Indiscriminate use of water in the garden is now seen as unacceptably wasteful. Careful watering, however, results in a healthy and more sustainable garden.

What to water Give young plants a thorough watering after planting and until they establish; they will usually need less water later on. In summer, pots and baskets need watering regularly, and vegetable gardens must be kept moist to continue cropping. Beds and borders should be watered only during periods of drought.

How to water In summer, it is best to water either in the morning or evening, when it is cooler and less moisture is lost to evaporation. If you are spot-watering a particular plant or watering containers, use a watering can rather than a hose, so that the water can be applied more carefully. If you are using a hose to water borders, remember that frequent light waterings have less benefit than an occasional good soak. It is even thought that frequent watering encourages roots to grow closer to the soil surface, making plants dry out more quickly. Rather than spray water over plants, hold the hose, or watering can, close to the base of the plant, allowing water to soak down well into the soil.

Water plants thoroughly when first planted.

Spraying a plant's leaves will not water it properly.

A seep hose will deliver water to a plant easily and efficiently.

Water-efficient methods

The simplest way to make your watering more efficient is to remove soil from around the base of a plant, to form a shallow depression. This then fills with water and prevents wasteful run-off. Alternatively, sink a pot or length of pipe into the soil next to a plant. Filled with water, it delivers moisture close to the roots where it is required. For plants that need plenty of moisture, a seep hose (*left*) delivers water gently and efficiently over several hours. Mulches, drought-tolerant plants, and avoiding overly dense planting further reduces the need for watering.

Once installed, automatic watering systems can save time and water.

Automatic systems

These watering systems are particularly useful in smaller gardens, or if you are often away or have little time to water your plants by hand. They usually involve networks of narrow tubing, connected to a small timer that is attached to a tap. At pre-set times, the timer switches on and off, and water flows through the pipes. Attached to the pipes are seep hoses or mini sprinklers (*left*) that spout water around the plants in pots or in borders. These systems are sometimes fiddly to install and seem expensive initially, but they are ideal for areas that will not be disturbed by digging.

Feeding and staking your plants

To keep plants healthy, you will need to feed them with fertilizers. This is particularly important for plants growing in containers. As the season progresses, many herbaceous plants in borders require some extra support to keep them looking tidy.

Choosing fertilizers

Different fertilizers are designed for a range of situations, offering differing ratios of nutrients and methods of application. Choosing the most suitable plant feed for your needs will result in improved plant performance.

Organic fertilizers Bulky materials, such as garden compost and manure, as well as concentrated feeds, such as bone meal and dried seaweed meal, are good long-term sources of nitrogen. They supply fewer nutrients than inorganic fertilizers, however, although bulky types also improve the soil. Concentrated organic fertilizers are easy to apply and release nutrients slowly.

Inorganic fertilizers These contain higher concentrations of nutrients and are relatively light and easy to apply. They are also good value and fast-acting, ideal for plants showing symptoms of a nutrient deficiency. Being soluble, they are easily washed through sandy soils.

Liquid feeds Good for plants in containers, liquid feeds – which also come in powder form – are mixed with water in a watering can, or applied using a special fitting attached to a hose that will deliver an even dose.

Slow-release granular feeds Relatively expensive but ideal for potted plants, these usually come in tablet stick or granular form and are designed to release their nutrients gradually, usually over several months.

Potash fertilizers These feeds are rich in potassium, a nutrient required in large amounts by most plants. Fruit and vegetables may need a high-potash feed, since too little potassium reduces yields.

Nitrogen-rich fertilizers Nitrogen is vital for lush, healthy plant growth. Nitrogen-rich fertilizers often contain a high percentage of ammonium nitrate. Organic fertilizers, such as pelleted chicken manure or dried blood, are also a good source of nitrogen.

Signs of a poor diet Yellowing or pale foliage, especially at the margins of the leaves, as well as generally slow, lacklustre, or spindly growth are indications that a plant may need feeding. Plants may also fail to flower or fruit properly. Nitrogen or potassium deficiencies are the most common causes and are easily treated with fertilizer.

When to feed Apply feed during the growing season, when plants will absorb and benefit from the nutrients. Start to reduce feeding towards the end of the summer. Avoid feeding in very dry conditions; the best time to apply is when the soil is moist. Fertilizers applied in winter will not be absorbed and are usually washed away.

Plants that need staking Many herbaceous perennials tend to grow taller in fertile garden conditions than in the wild. They become top-heavy, flopping over just as they begin to bloom. Other plants, developed by breeders for larger flowers, suffer from similar problems. Flopping can make borders look unkempt but is easily solved using stakes and supports, such as canes, wires and netting, to hold stems up and keep clumps of plants together. Position any supports early in the growing season in spring, preferably before the plants emerge, so that growth will pass through and mask them as it develops. Supports added later usually appear unsightly, although they may still be required, especially after heavy rain or high winds.

- *Achillea*
- *Agapanthus*
- *Aster* 'Coombe Fishacre'
- *Aster turbinellus*
- *Astrantia major*
- *Catananche caerulea*
- *Dahlia*
- *Delphinium*
- *Dicentra spectabilis*
- *Echinacea purpurea*
- *Gaura lindheimeri*
- *Geum coccineum*
- *Helenium* 'Moerheim Beauty'
- *Lupinus*
- *Penstemon*
- *Persicaria*
- *Phlox*
- *Rudbeckia*
- *Sedum* 'Herbstfreude'

Proprietary stakes and rings Purpose-made supports, such as wire hoops on legs, or angled stakes that link together, are useful in the garden. Usually green, they are easily hidden by foliage. Supports should be installed in spring, but sometimes they may be needed later when a plant collapses and leaves a gaping hole in a border.

Invisible supports One of the best types of invisible support is fine green netting stretched taut over the crowns of plants, such as asters, and held by a series of wooden stakes about 50cm (20in) tall. Stake in early spring so the shoots grow through and disguise the netting, and plants have a firm support when they bloom.

Ways to weed

Weeding is usually regarded as a dull, joyless chore, but controlling these unwanted plants is an important part of keeping your garden looking its best and your plants healthy and in good condition.

Why weed? It is often said that a weed is nothing more than a plant in the wrong place. This is true but, given the chance, many common weeds will quickly overrun a garden, out-competing prized plants for light, water, and nutrients, thanks to their ability to colonize rapidly. As well as making your beds look unsightly, many weeds harbour pests and diseases that can be spread around the garden. Putting in the effort to remove weeds will pay off eventually; after a few years, the time you spend weeding will be greatly reduced.

Suppressing weed growth In a well-stocked garden, weeding is less of a chore than in a young plot with big gaps and empty borders. This is because ground-covering garden plants help to prevent weed seedlings from germinating and taking hold. Perennial weeds are a more serious problem and may take some years to kill off. If you are planting a large area, it is often worth considering a geo-textile membrane, which eliminates light and hinders the growth of perennial weeds. The membrane is laid over the soil and then covered with a mulch at planting time.

Hoeing weeds A garden hoe is a useful tool for removing young weed seedlings from flower beds since it enables you to reach deep into a border without trampling on the soil. Pass the hoe briskly through the soil, just beneath the surface, lifting weeds by severing their roots.

Chemical controls Perennial weeds, such as bindweed and ground elder, may seem indestructible, since they will grow from the tiniest section of root left in the soil. Spraying with a systemic herbicide containing chemicals that are relayed to the roots is one way to eradicate them.

Clearing a lawn The simplest way to remove lawn weeds is to extract them with a fork, kitchen knife, or daisy grubber. You may need to treat tougher weeds, such as large dandelions, with a lawn weedkiller. Badly affected turf may respond well to a "feed and weed" treatment.

Tackling perennial weeds The best solution for a border overrun with perennial weeds may be to dig it by hand to remove every bit of root, or to apply weedkiller – either spot-applied to individual weeds or to the whole bed after all ornamentals have been removed.

Weed troubleshooter

Weeds are an unfortunate fact of life in the garden, but by weeding from the start of the first growing season, you will gradually reduce the number that appear year on year. More persistent weeds may need special treatment: here's a guide to the worst offenders and how to eradicate them for good.

Bindweed
This twining climber scrambles over plants and chokes them. Wiry stems, heart-shaped leaves, and white or pink, trumpet-shaped flowers are produced by a network of white roots that spread through the soil. The smallest piece of root produces a shoot. Dig out the roots or treat the shoots by painting on a herbicide.

Stinging nettle
The stinging hairs on the foliage can make brushes with this weed painful. Small plants often lurk undetected in borders. Perennial nettles spread quickly just under the soil via thin runners, which soon form new plants. Dig out the plant (wearing gloves), ensuring that all runners and young plants are removed.

Horsetail
This primitive plant has rather delicate-looking stems attached to black roots that run very deep and break easily, only to regrow weeks later. If you have a single plant, keep removing the top growth to weaken and eventually kill it. For bad infestations, dig over the soil, remove all roots, and treat any regrowth with a herbicide.

Dock
With its soft, lush foliage, dock is a large weed often found in beds and borders, and sometimes in grass. It grows from a long, deep tap root that snaps off easily and must be removed from the soil to prevent the plant from regrowing. Keep removing the top growth to kill single plants, or treat with a paint-on herbicide.

Japanese knotweed
A pernicious weed with fast-growing, rather attractive stems up to 2m (6ft) tall, clothed densely with lush, heart-shaped leaves. It has a tough, rampaging rootstock and the tiniest piece of root can form a new colony. Repeated applications of herbicide and removal of plants as they appear may eventually prove effective.

Ground elder
A low-growing weed, often found in borders, that produces taller stems and white flowers in summer. Thin white runners spread through the soil and new plants quickly carpet the ground. Use a hand fork to remove as much plant material as possible, trying not to break up the roots too much. Treat severe cases with herbicide.

Dandelion
Common in borders and lawns, the dandelion, with its distinctive yellow flowers and fluffy seedheads, has a long tap root that snaps easily when you try to remove the plant, only to regrow. Small plants, especially those in lawns, can be dug out with a daisy grubber. Established plants may need treating with a paint-on herbicide.

Oxalis
This little weed looks like a clover, with green or purple foliage, and is usually found in cracks in paving. It spreads like wildfire, using explosive seed pods. Although easily pulled, the roots leave behind little bulbils that regrow into more plants. Remove as many as possible, then treat any new plants with a herbicide.

Common ragwort
Usually found in lawns, this weed is a biennial or short-lived perennial that has hairy, rather malodorous leaves with ruffled margins. Yellow daisy-like flowers appear on tall stems and are cut by mowing. It is unsightly and poisonous to livestock. Pull out the rosettes by hand or with a daisy grubber before the plant sets seed.

Bramble
This large, woody weed is usually only a problem in neglected gardens that need clearing. Its long, arching stems are covered in savage barbs and their tips root in the ground to form new plants. Old, deep-rooted plants can be difficult to extract. Remove as much material as possible by hand; use a herbicide in severe cases.

Herb Robert
A wild geranium, this annual or short-lived perennial spreads freely from seed. Its purplish-green mature foliage is slightly sticky and has a nasty smell. Small purple flowers appear in summer. These weeds can lurk amid taller plants in borders and form quite a population. Pull them up by hand before they set seed.

Dealing with pests

Many popular garden plants are prone to attacks by pests, which can cause damage and even death.

Looking after your plants can deter pests, but as a last resort, combat severe infestations with pesticides.

Deterring pests Healthy plants are less prone to attack from pests and, if affected, are better able to withstand the ill-effects. Make sure that plants introduced into the garden are pest- and disease-free and that established specimens are well tended. Choose robust plants that seldom fall prey to pests, and avoid growing similar species in the same spot for too long, especially soft fruit and vegetables. Remove weeds and garden rubbish, which may be home to pests such as slugs and snails. Protect vulnerable plants using traps (beer traps for slugs, for example) or physical barriers: cut the bottoms off clear plastic drinks bottles and place them over young plants to help protect them (*right*).

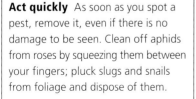

Act quickly As soon as you spot a pest, remove it, even if there is no damage to be seen. Clean off aphids from roses by squeezing them between your fingers; pluck slugs and snails from foliage and dispose of them.

Encourage friendly predators Some insects and garden visitors eat pests, so welcome them. A few logs in a corner will shelter ground beetles and may encourage hedgehogs, which feed on slugs and snails.

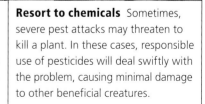

Resort to chemicals Sometimes, severe pest attacks may threaten to kill a plant. In these cases, responsible use of pesticides will deal swiftly with the problem, causing minimal damage to other beneficial creatures.

Common pests

Vine weevils The white larvae eat the roots of many plants, causing them to collapse; black adult weevils eat notches out of foliage.

Capsid bugs Green or brown in colour, these insects suck plant sap and kill plant tissues, distorting the shoot tips of many plants in summer.

Sawfly The green or brown caterpillar-like larvae of these insects strip the foliage of plants, such as roses and gooseberries, in early summer.

Earwigs These creatures often target dahlias, living in and damaging the blooms in late summer. They also eat the young leaves of other plants.

Ants When ants build their nests in the lawn or in planted containers, they may affect plant growth and become a nuisance.

Lily beetles A real problem for lily growers, both red adult beetles and the young slimy black grubs devour lily foliage and flowers in summer.

Aphids Also called greenfly or blackfly, these sap-suckers affect many plants, especially roses, distorting growth and spreading disease.

Flea beetles These tiny black beetles produce tiny holes and white spots on leaves, especially of brassicas. In severe cases, seedlings die.

Slugs and snails The best known of garden pests, these voracious feeders eat soft plant material, usually at night, decimating plants such as hostas.

Preventing diseases

When plants look unwell and there is no sign of any pests, a plant disease may be the cause. There are ways to minimize the risk of disease, and if you can identify common problems, you should be able to treat plants quickly.

Keeping plants healthy Diseases are often worse when plants are in poor health or under stress through lack of water or nourishment, so keep your garden in the best condition possible. When buying a new plant, check that it is healthy and suited to its intended position. This, coupled with good aftercare, should prevent problems later.

Removing contaminants An important part of good plant husbandry is to keep the garden tidy. This includes removing and disposing of diseased plant material, such as fallen rose leaves infected with black spot. Old, fallen foliage can cause further infection, as spores released from the fungus on the leaf are spread about on the air.

Prevention and cure While keeping plants in good health and removing materials that may harbour disease can help to prevent outbreaks, sometimes the only option is to use a chemical, such as a fungicide, to cure infected plants. A combination of prevention and cure is usually the best way to deal with plant diseases.

Tackling viruses Viruses can occur in almost any plant, usually causing distorted foliage growth or strange colour breaks in flowers. The virus particles are present in the sap of infected plants and can be spread by aphids. Affected plants are usually destroyed.

Common diseases

Black spot A fungal disease spread by splashing rain, or on the air, causing round black spots, sometimes with yellow margins, on leaves. Chemical controls are effective, and good plant care and hygiene important.

Coral spot This fungus causes shoots to die back on trees and shrubs. Orange pustules on stems release disease-spreading spores. Remove affected growth and any debris, disinfecting pruning equipment before each cut.

Botrytis Also called grey mould, this fungus often affects soft young plants, causing furry, grey growth and the eventual collapse of the plant. Remove affected material promptly and improve air circulation.

Powdery mildew This silvery-white fungus affects the leaves of many plants, which eventually yellow and then fall. Dry conditions are often to blame, so keep plants moist and spray with a suitable fungicide if necessary.

Rust A fungal disease, this produces orange patches on the undersides of leaves, causing them to fall early. Remove infected material, improve air circulation, and spray with a suitable fungicide.

Rhododendron bud blast A fungus that prevents rhododendron flower buds from opening, turning them black with furry growth. Remove affected buds promptly.

Plant guide

The following plants are all suitable for small gardens, and have been grouped according to their height and sun requirements. Many have the RHS Award of Garden Merit, which means that they are excellent plants for garden use.

Key to plant symbols

⚘ Plants given the RHS Award of Garden Merit

Soil preference

◌ Well-drained soil

◓ Moist soil

● Wet soil

Preference for sun or shade

☼ Full sun

◐ Partial or dappled shade

☀ Full shade

Hardiness ratings

❊❊❊ Fully hardy plants

❊❊ Plants that survive outside in mild regions or sheltered sites

❊ Plants that need protection from frost over winter

❀ Tender plants that do not tolerate any degree of frost

Tall plants for sun (Ab–Cy)

Abutilon *x* suntense
This spectacular evergreen shrub is a fine choice for a sunny, sheltered site by a wall or fence. The hairy, grey-green leaves are shaped like those of a grapevine. In late spring, clusters of large, open, purple or white flowers cover the plant for many weeks.

H: 4m (12ft), **S**: 2m (6ft)
❋❋ ◊ ☼

Acacia dealbata
Reaching tree-sized proportions, this quick-growing evergreen has fern-like, sea-green foliage. In sheltered spots, it produces scented, puffball-shaped, yellow flowers in late winter. If it grows too large, it can be pruned to size in spring.

H: 15m (50ft), **S**: 6m (20ft)
❋❋ ◊ ☼ ♔

Arbutus unedo
The strawberry tree is one of the best evergreen trees for a small garden. Shrubby when young, it has glossy, dark green leaves and bell-shaped, white or pink flowers in late autumn, followed by strawberry-like fruits. The bark is reddish-brown.

H: 10m (30ft), **S**: 6m (20ft)
❋❋❋ ◊ ☼ ♔

Betula utilis *var.* jacquemontii
With its light canopy and slender form, this silver birch suits small sites well. In winter, the dazzling white trunk with its peeling bark provides interest; catkins and young leaves are an attraction in spring. The leaves turn butter-yellow before falling.

H: 15m (50ft), **S**: 7.5m (23ft)
❋❋❋ ◑ ◊ ☼ ☀

Buddleja davidii '*Dartmoor*'
Buddlejas are easy to grow and attractive to butterflies. In mid- to late summer this graceful selection has reddish-purple, cone-shaped flowerheads on long, arching stems, giving a weeping appearance. Prune in spring to keep under control.

H: 3m (10ft), **S**: 2m (6ft)
❋❋❋ ◊ ☼ ♔

Cestrum parqui
An unusual shrub that is ideal for a warm, sunny wall. Its greenish-yellow flowerheads, which are scented at night, appear from spring until the frosts. In cold areas, the plant may die to the ground, but will usually grow again from the root.

H: 3m (10ft), **S**: 2m (6ft)
❋❋ ◊ ☼ ♔

Clematis *'Alba Luxurians'*

One of the most rewarding clematis, this plant bears masses of small green-tipped white flowers with black anthers. Mature plants scramble up trellis to cover a wall or fence, but may overwhelm shrubs or small trees. In late winter, cut back to 20cm (8in).

H: 5m (14ft), **S**: 1.5m (5ft)
❄❄❄ ◊ ☼ ♈

Clematis cirrhosa

Both evergreen and winter-flowering, this scrambling climber needs a sunny position, but proves a quick-growing, easy plant. The shiny leaves make a good foil to the creamy, bell-shaped flowers, which can be speckled with red inside; fluffy seedheads follow.

H: 6m (20ft), **S**: 3m (10ft)
❄❄ ◊ ◊◊ ☼

Clematis *'Perle d'Azur'*

This plant makes an excellent addition to a small garden. It produces blue blooms in succession from midsummer to autumn. The flowers are tinged violet as they open, but fade to blue as they age. Prune stems to 20cm (8in) in late winter.

H: 3m (10ft), **S**: 1.5m (5ft)
❄❄❄ ◊ ☼

Cornus kousa *var.* chinensis

This must rank as one of the best garden plants. White or pink spring flowers with showy bracts are followed by red, strawberry-like fruits. Mature plants become more tree-like and the flower displays ever more spectacular.

H: 7m (22ft), **S**: 5m (15ft)
❄❄❄ ◊ ☼ ♈

Cotinus coggygria *'Royal Purple'*

For lovers of coloured foliage, this large shrub is a good choice. The rich red-purple leaves offset pale-coloured flowers at the back of a border. In summer, wispy flowerheads may be produced; in autumn, leaves gradually turn scarlet before falling.

H: 5m (15ft), **S**: 4m (12ft)
❄❄❄ ◊ ◊◊ ☼ ◐ ♈

Cynara cardunculus

The cardoon makes a fine plant even in small gardens, with its architectural form, silver-green foliage, and purple, thistle-like flowers, which attract bees. Place at the back of a border or use as a feature plant for a sunny corner. It dies to the ground in winter.

H: 2m (6ft), **S**: 1.2m (4ft)
❄❄ ◊ ☼ ♈

Tall plants for sun (Ja–Tr)

Jasminum nudiflorum

Of all winter-flowering plants, this jasmine, usually grown as a climber, is perhaps the most reliable. Small, bright yellow flowers appear all winter on leafless, dark green stems. Hard frost will claim some blooms, but more are produced in mild spells.

H: 4m (12ft), **S**: 4m (12ft)
❄❄❄ ◊ ◑ ☼ ◐ ♈ ♉

Juniperus communis 'Hibernica'

This conifer brings contrast, structure, and backbone to the small garden. With blue-green, prickly needles and a dense-growing, compact habit, it eventually forms a column several metres high, standing out from rounded and horizontal growth.

H: 5m (15ft), **S**: 60cm (24in)
❄❄❄ ◊ ◑ ☼ ◐ ♈ ♉

Mahonia x media 'Buckland'

A useful shrub with glossy evergreen foliage, architectural form, and sweetly scented, bright yellow flowers held in spikes during the darkest winter months. The leaves are spiny; weeding beneath these plants is best done wearing gloves.

H: 4m (12ft), **S**: 3m (10ft)
❄❄❄ ◊ ◑ ☼ ◐ ♈ ♉

Malus 'John Downie'

This compact crab apple is perhaps the best of its kind for a profusion of ornamental fruit in late summer. Yellow and orange in colour, and large, the apples stand out from the deciduous foliage. In spring, pure white blossom opens from pink buds.

H: 10m (30ft), **S**: 6m (20ft)
❄❄❄ ◑ ☼ ◐ ♉

Olea europaea

The olive has become viable for temperate gardens, thanks to milder winters. It needs a sheltered site and as much sun as possible. It then makes a noble specimen with evergreen, silver-green foliage and a grey trunk. Small white flowers appear in summer.

H: 6m (20ft), **S**: 5m (15ft)
❄❄ ◊ ☼

Photinia x fraseri 'Red Robin'

Evergreen photinia is at its glorious best in spring when the new bright copper-red growth appears; the large, smooth leaves retain a reddish tinge as they mature. It can be used as a hedge, since it responds well to pruning, and is quite compact.

H: 3m (10ft), **S**: 3m (10ft)
❄❄ ◑ ☼ ◐ ♉

Prunus *x* subhirtella *'Autumnalis Rosea'*

This tree suits those who like to enjoy the garden all year. Delicate, starry, pale pink flowers are produced between autumn and spring. New spring growth is bronze-green, turning dark green as the leaves expand.

H: 8m (25ft), **S**: 6m (20ft)
❋❋❋ ◊ ◖ ☼ ♈

Robinia pseudoacacia *'Frisia'*

This deciduous tree's golden foliage provides dramatic contrast to other plants and illuminates dark town gardens. Plants are usually grafted and have thorny, brittle stems; remove any suckers with green leaves that appear from the base.

H: 15m (50ft), **S**: 8m (25ft)
❋❋❋ ◖ ☼ ♈

Romneya coulteri

The tree poppy is a distinguished perennial that sends up tall yet slender, unbranched stems with silvery leaves that in mid- to late summer are topped by huge, scented, gold-centred flowers with delicate white petals.

H: 2m (6ft), **S**: 2m (6ft)
❋❋❋ ◊ ☼ ♈

Solanum crispum *'Glasnevin'*

This glamorous relation of the potato has scrambling stems, and makes a beautiful wall shrub. Small purple flowers with yellow centres appear in bunches all summer and associate well with clematis and roses. Plants respond well to a light trim in spring.

H: 4m (12ft), **S**: 2m (6ft)
❋❋ ◊ ☼ ♈

Sorbus cashmiriana

With its open growth habit, delicate foliage, and pink flowerheads in early summer, this tree is a good choice. In autumn and early winter, the canopy is resplendent with clusters of shiny white fruits the size of small marbles that linger after the leaves have fallen.

H: 8m (25ft), **S**: 6m (20ft)
❋❋❋ ◊ ◖ ☼ ◑ ♈

Trachelospermum asiaticum

This evergreen climber is an excellent plant for the smaller garden; it does best in a sheltered spot. Small glossy leaves form dense cover up walls or over fences, and from early summer, clusters of starry, strongly scented cream flowers appear.

H: 4m (12ft), **S**: 3m (10ft)
❋❋ ◊ ◖ ☼ ◑ ♈

Tall plants for shade (Ac–St)

Acer palmatum *var.* dissectum
Dissectum Atropurpureum Group
This is one of the most popular of small Japanese acers, with rich purple foliage. Slow-growing, it eventually forms a low, mounded shrub. The delicate leaves may be damaged by drying winds, so give it some shelter.

H: 2m (6ft), **S**: 3m (10ft)
✽✽✽ ◊ ◗ ☼

Camellia sasanqua
Most camellias bloom in spring but those of *C. sasanqua* open in late autumn. There are many cultivars, with scented single or semi-double flowers in white or pink. Train stems against a sheltered wall to protect the flowers from frost. Needs acid soil.

H: 4m (12ft), **S**: 2m (6ft)
✽✽✽ ◊ ◗ ☼ ☼

Cercis canadensis '*Forest Pansy*'
One of the most desirable of all deciduous shrubs, this is grown for its heart-shaped, rich purple foliage and clusters of purple, pea-like flowers in spring. In autumn, the leaves develop orange tints before falling. Grow it in a sheltered position.

H: 3m (10ft), **S**: 3m (10ft)
✽✽✽ ◗ ☼ ☼ ♖

Daphne bholua '*Jacqueline Postill*'
It is worth spending time finding a good spot for this evergreen daphne. In winter, it bears a profusion of waxy pink flowers with an intoxicating perfume that carries on the wind. It is best planted in a sheltered spot.

H: 3m (10ft), **S**: 1.5m (5ft)
✽✽ ◊ ◗ ☼ ♖

Dicksonia antarctica
This tree fern is one of the most recognizable of exotic plants. Its bright green fronds unfurl from tight croziers that appear from the tip of the slow-growing trunk. These plants need shelter, moisture, and protection in cold winters.

H: 6m (20ft), **S**: 4m (13ft)
✽✽ ◗ ☼ ♖

Fatsia japonica
Few hardy plants provide more impact than fatsia, with its large, leathery, hand-shaped leaves. In autumn, heads of white flowers are followed by drooping bunches of shiny, black berries. It develops an elegant, upright habit with age.

H: 3m (10ft), **S**: 2m (6ft)
✽✽ ◊ ◗ ☼ ☼ ♖

Hydrangea quercifolia

Most hydrangeas are grown for their showy flowerheads, but this species is better known for its oak-like foliage, which develops dramatic autumnal colours before falling. Creamy-white, conical flowerheads are long-lasting. It remains a compact shrub.

H: 1.5m (5ft), **S**: 1m (3ft)
❁❁❁ ◊ ☼ ◖ ♛

Ilex aquifolium 'Silver Queen'

This slow-growing holly is a reliable performer. It eventually forms a large, cone-shaped shrub with prickly evergreen leaves edged with silver. An undemanding shrub for a dark corner or shaded border, it is a male plant and will not produce berries.

H: 12m (40ft), **S**: 3m (10ft) or more
❁❁❁ ◊ ◖ ☼ ◖ ♛

Lonicera periclymenum 'Graham Thomas'

This is one of the best honeysuckles. It is shade-tolerant, free-flowering, and well scented, especially in the evening. Creamy-yellow, tubular flowers appear in early summer and throughout the season.

H: 4m (12ft), **S**: 3m (10ft)
❁❁❁ ◊ ◖ ☼ ◖ ♛

Phyllostachys

Beloved of garden designers, this bamboo is an excellent, well-behaved, clump-forming plant. *P. nigra* has rich ebony stems that contrast well with the bright green foliage. Remove lower branchlets and older stems to show off the colour of the stems.

H: 7m (22ft), **S**: 5m (15ft)
❁❁❁ ◊ ◖ ☼ ◖ ♛

Sambucus racemosa 'Plumosa Aurea'

In spring and summer, this deciduous shrub is furnished with delicate, gold feathery foliage; the young shoots are tinged bronze. It is best if the stems are cut down annually to about 60cm (24in) in early spring.

H: 3m (10ft), **S**: 2m (6ft)
❁❁❁ ◊ ◖ ☼ ◖

Stewartia monadelpha

Stewartias are deciduous trees, often developing mottled trunks and impressive autumnal tints before leaf fall. This species is one of the more widely available, producing white summer flowers like those of a small camellia. Grow it in a sheltered spot.

H: 20m (70ft), **S**: 5m (15ft)
❁❁❁ ◊ ☼ ◖

Medium-sized plants for sun (Ac–Co)

Acanthus mollis
With mounds of glossy architectural foliage and handsome prickly spires of purple flowers, this perennial will add a touch of drama to any garden. The large, rich green leaves that emerge in early spring may be damaged by frosts.

H: 2m (6ft), **S**: 2m (6ft)
❀❀ ◊ ☼ ☀ ♈

Allium hollandicum
'Purple Sensation'
This bulb flowers after the spring bulbs but before summer flowers get going. Rounded, metallic purple flowerheads are carried on tall, slender stems that punctuate lower plantings. Plant in drifts in spring.

H: 1.2m (4ft), **S**: 20cm (8in)
❀❀❀ ◊ ☼ ♈ ♉

Angelica archangelica
This herbaceous plant flowers, sets seed, and dies in two years. In its first year, it produces unremarkable clumps of large, divided leaves, but in the second year, it is transformed. A stout stem is topped by football-sized heads composed of bright green flowers.

H: 2.5m (8ft), **S**: 1.2m (4ft)
❀❀❀ ◊ ☼ ☀

Aster turbinellus
Reaching its best in early autumn, this aster has mauve daisy flowers held aloft on slender stems. The yellow-centred blooms are produced in profusion, creating a dainty effect. The stems may need extra support; position any canes or twigs early.

H: 1m (3ft), **S**: 1m (3ft)
❀❀❀ ◊ ◊ ☼ ♉

Berberis thunbergii f.
atropurpurea *'Dart's Red Lady'*
Berberis are tough and easy to grow, but some make first-rate flowering or foliage plants. This deciduous cultivar with viciously spiny stems is grown for its richly coloured red leaves, making a good foil for other garden plants.

H: 1.2m (4ft), **S**: 2m (6ft)
❀❀❀ ◊ ◊ ☼ ☀

Bupleurum fruticosum
This is a fine shrub for a sunny spot, forming a mound of silver-green evergreen foliage, and producing delicate heads of tiny, bright yellow flowers all summer. It thrives in dry, chalky soil and also in the open in mild coastal areas.

H: 2m (6ft), **S**: 2m (6ft)
❀❀ ◊ ☼

Buxus sempervirens

Box has a long history in cultivation, thanks to its evergreen nature and good response to clipping. Use as topiary, a low hedge, or shape it to add formality. 'Marginata' (pictured) has yellow-edged leaves. Dislikes waterlogged soil.

H: 3–4m (10–12ft) if unclipped,
S: 2m (6ft) ❄❄❄ ◐ ◑ ☼ ◑ ♀

Canna 'Striata'

Thanks to their exotic flowers and bold foliage, cannas make great plants for a sunny garden. 'Striata' has yellow-striped green leaves and orange flowers in summer. Lift the rhizomes and keep frost-free, or protect with a thick mulch in winter.

H: 2m (6ft), **S**: 1m (3ft)
❄ ◐ ☼ ♀

Chimonanthus praecox

In summer, this deciduous shrub is unremarkable; in winter, small rounded buds swell and open to waxy, creamy-yellow, bell-shaped flowers with a purple centre. Their spicy perfume gives the plants its common name of wintersweet.

H: 3m (10ft), **S**: 2m (6ft)
❄❄❄ ◐ ☼

Choisya ternata Sundance

This neat shrub is popular due to its golden evergreen foliage, which is lightly aromatic, as are the sprays of white flowers. It is best grown in some shade when it becomes lime-green and has an illuminating presence. Dislikes waterlogged soil.

H: 2m (6ft), **S**: 1.5m (5ft)
❄❄ ◐ ☼ ◑ ♀

Cistus x hybridus

This easy, evergreen shrub is a sight to behold in early summer. For two to three weeks, it is smothered in masses of single, white flowers with a yellow eye. Cistus are not long-lived, but they will endure drought for a while.

H: 1.2m (4ft), **S**: 1.5m (5ft)
❄❄ ◐ ☼

Correa 'Dusky Bells'

This charming, winter-flowering plant is worth growing in a sheltered, sunny position. Low and shrubby, it has small, evergreen leaves and bears pinkish-red, bell-shaped flowers with protruding anthers in mild spells during winter. It needs shelter.

H: 1m (3ft), **S**: 60cm (24in)
❄❄ ◐ ◑ ☼ ♀

Medium-sized plants for sun (Cr–Hi)

Crocosmia x crocosmiiflora 'Venus'

The common montbretia has strappy leaves topped by sprays of orange flowers in late summer, but there are many rather more desirable selections. C. x crocosmiiflora 'Venus', with gold and red flowers, is a good example.

H: 50cm (20in), **S**: 60cm (24in)
✸✸ ◊ ◗ ☼ ☀

Dahlia 'Bishop of Llandaff'

This popular old cultivar produces velvety, red, single flowers above purple foliage. It is compact, making it good for the smaller plot, and a fine companion for other late-flowering perennials. Lift the plant in winter and keep the tubers frost-free.

H: 1.2m (4ft), **S**: 60cm (24in)
✸ ◗ ☼ ♈

Deutzia x rosea 'Campanulata'

This compact, deciduous shrub makes a good undemanding plant for the smaller garden. It has upright, twiggy growth and hairy leaves. The blooms, which are bell-shaped and white with a pink tinge, remain beautiful for several weeks.

H: 1.2m (4ft), **S**: 1.2m (4ft)
✸✸✸ ◊ ◗ ☼ ☀

Dierama pulcherrimum

The wand flower or angel's fishing rod is aptly named. In summer, long arching sprays of large, bell-shaped flowers appear from tufts of tough, strappy, evergreen leaves. Flowers are usually pink but sometimes white or even dark purple.

H: 1.5m (5ft), **S**: 60cm (24in)
✸✸ ◗ ☼

Echinacea purpurea

The cone flower is a most appealing herbaceous plant, producing pinky-purple daisy-like flowers with a large, dark central cone, tinged orange. The flowers are held on stout stems, although sideshoots carry later blooms that appear well into autumn.

H: 1.2m (4ft), **S**: 60cm (24in)
✸✸✸ ◊ ☼

Euphorbia characias

This evergreen perennial is a superb early summer-flowering plant, with rounded heads of lime-green bracts surrounding insignificant flowers. The sea-green, lance-shaped leaves are carried on fleshy stems that bleed a milky toxic sap if cut.

H: 1.5m (5ft), **S**: 1m (3ft)
✸✸ ◊ ◗ ☼

Euphorbia x martinii

This spurge is a good choice, being of compact but upright growth and particularly effective in flower. The green blooms have red centres and appear in spring on tall, rounded, airy heads, carried on purple stems with dark evergreen leaves.

H: 60cm (24in), **S**: 60cm (24in)
❀❀❀ ◊ ☼ ♈

Grevillea 'Canberra Gem'

For much of the year, this unusual evergreen shrub is quietly attractive, clad in narrow, almost needle-like, bright green leaves. In summer, it is transformed with exotic-looking, pink-red flowers dangling here and there. It needs acidic soil.

H: 1.5m (5ft), **S**: 1.5m (5ft)
❀❀ ◊ ☼ ♈

Hebe 'Midsummer Beauty'

The length of its floral display makes this evergreen hebe worthy of space in the garden. In midsummer, long spikes of violet and white flowers are produced. They have a delicate fragrance and continue into autumn, even winter, if the weather is mild.

H: 2m (6ft), **S**: 2m (6ft)
❀❀ ◊ ◑ ☼ ◐ ♈

Helenium 'Moerheim Beauty'

This late-flowering border perennial is deservedly popular. From mid- to late summer to early autumn, it produces shuttlecock-shaped, daisy-like flowers in rich marmalade shades on stout upright stems. Deadheading ensures a later flush of blooms.

H: 1.4m (4½ft), **S**: 1m (3ft)
❀❀❀ ◊ ◑ ☼ ♈

Hemerocallis 'Corky'

A clump-forming perennial with narrow, strappy foliage. Slender stems appear in summer, carrying clusters of orange-yellow, funnel-shaped flowers, each displaying a red tinge to the outside. The blooms last just a day but are soon followed by others.

H: 60cm (24in), **S**: 60cm (24in)
❀❀❀ ◊ ◑ ☼ ◐ ♈

Hibiscus syriacus 'Oiseau Bleu'

Few shrubs better this hibiscus in full bloom. Just as many other plants are fading, it produces a profusion of 8cm- (3in-) wide, open bell-shaped flowers of rich blue – a rare colour so late in the season. The flowers last until early autumn.

H: 2.5m (8ft), **S**: 1.5m (5ft)
❀❀❀ ◊ ☼ ♈

Medium-sized plants for sun (In–Ph)

Inula hookeri

This clump-forming perennial should be more widely grown. It produces beautiful yellow flowers with slender petals that appear from midsummer at the tips of soft stems bearing hairy oval leaves. In late autumn, the shoots can be cut to the ground.

H: 60cm (24in), **S**: 60cm (24in)
❁❁❁ ◊ ☼ ☀

Iris laevigata

This plant is perfect for moist areas, growing well even in standing water. The sword-shaped foliage provides a contrast to other shrubby growth. In early to midsummer, flowering stems bear a succession of beautiful blooms, usually lavender-blue in colour.

H: 50cm (20in), **S**: 30cm (12in)
❁❁❁ ◊ ◖ ☼ ☀ ♈

Iris sibirica 'Perry's Blue'

Siberian irises are good for ground that does not dry out. In spring, slender, strappy foliage erupts from clumps, followed by tall, branched, flowering stems. These bear dainty sky-blue flowers with white markings, 6cm (2½in) across, over several weeks.

H: 1m (3ft), **S**: 50cm (20in)
❁❁❁ ◊ ◖ ☼ ☀

Lavandula stoechas

With its aromatic foliage and long-lasting flowers, French lavender lends a Mediterranean feel to sunny gardens. The flowerheads have distinctive purple "ears", or bracts, held on stems above the narrow, greyish-green leaves. Grow in a sheltered spot.

H: 60cm (24in), **S**: 60cm (24in)
❁❁ ◊ ☼ ♈

Lilium regale

This is an easy lily to grow. Fleshy stems furnished with narrow leaves appear in spring and grow rapidly. Large buds swell and burst to reveal silver-white, trumpet-shaped flowers with protruding stamens and a wonderful scent.

H: 1.5m (5ft), **S**: 30cm (12in)
❁❁❁ ◊ ☼ ☀ ♈

Lobelia tupa

In spring, this exotic-looking plant produces fleshy, red-flushed shoots with large, rather downy leaves. In late summer, heads of red, tubular flowers open over several weeks, and last well into autumn. Cut stems to the ground after the first frosts.

H: 2m (6ft), **S**: 1m (3ft)
❁❁ ◊ ◖ ☼

Melianthus major

A remarkable foliage plant, with dramatic, blue-silver, deeply cut leaves that look superb in a white border or with contrasting purple foliage. Usually it is cut to the ground by frost, and should be covered with a thick mulch to protect the roots.

H: 2m (6ft), **S**: 1m (3ft)
❋❋ ◊ ◊ ☼ ♈

Miscanthus sinensis 'Zebrinus'

With its tall stems and strappy foliage, this ornamental grass is a favourite. The leaf blades are marked with broad yellow stripes, giving the plant a remarkable appearance, especially when grown in full sun, which helps intensify the markings.

H: 2m (6ft), **S**: 1m (3ft)
❋❋❋ ◑ ☼ ◐

Nandina domestica

A most useful shrub, this plant ticks all the boxes. It has a delicate yet architectural form with large, divided leaves that develop attractive autumnal tints. In early summer, sprays of white flowers appear, followed by clusters of orange berries that persist into winter.

H: 2m (6ft), **S**: 2m (6ft)
❋❋❋ ◊ ☼ ◑ ☼ ♈

Pennisetum setaceum 'Rubrum'

This delightful grass is a tender perennial, ideal for a container in a sunny spot during summer. Best treated as an annual, it will produce purple fluffy flowerheads (known as "cats' tails") held on arching stems, above rich red foliage.

H: 1m (3ft), **S**: 60cm (24in)
🏠 ◊ ◊ ☼

Perovskia 'Blue Spire'

This delicate-looking, shrubby plant is a good choice for a sunny, dry position. It forms an upright bush with strongly aromatic, silver-green foliage. From late summer until autumn, clouds of violet-blue flowers are produced.

H: 1.2m (4ft), **S**: 1m (3ft)
❋❋❋ ◊ ☼ ♈

Phlomis russeliana

A dependable, useful perennial with large, soft, heart-shaped leaves that cover the ground well, even in winter. In early summer, attractive stout stems of soft yellow flowers appear. After flowering, these stems provide structure into autumn and winter.

H: 1m (3ft), **S**: 1.2m (4ft)
❋❋❋ ◊ ◊ ☼ ◑ ♈

Medium-sized plants for sun (Ph–We)

Phormium 'Yellow Wave'

This tried-and-tested phormium is graceful and compact. Its broad, evergreen, strappy foliage is lavishly marked with yellow, set against green, each blade arching gracefully to give established clumps an elegant appearance.

H: 1.2m (4ft), **S**: 1m (3ft)
❄❄ ◊ ◖ ☼ ◖ ♈

Pinus mugo 'Ophir'

This compact, slow-growing pine is ideal for the smaller garden, growing well even in a container. Its short branching stems are covered in dense bristles and it will form a large shrub. However, it is most attractive in winter when its needles turn bright gold.

H: 1.5m (5ft), **S**: 1.5m (5ft)
❄❄❄ ◊ ☼

Pittosporum tobira

With its shiny, evergreen leaves and heads of cream-coloured, sweetly scented summer flowers, this plant should be seen more often. It grows throughout the Mediterranean, so is a good choice for those who like to be reminded of warmer climes.

H: 2m (6ft), **S**: 2m (6ft)
❄❄ ◊ ☼ ♈

Rosa x odorata 'Mutabilis'

A most beautiful rose that flowers from late spring until late autumn. Clusters of dainty, single flowers open a warm orange-yellow and turn rich pink with age. The young stems and leaves of this compact, but open, bush are tinged purple.

H: 1m (3ft), **S**: 1m (3ft)
❄❄ ◊ ☼ ♈

Rosa xanthina 'Canary Bird'

This rose is one of the earliest to bloom – in late spring. It produces a profusion of single, sunshine-yellow flowers, which have a light perfume, and has attractive apple-green foliage. A second reduced display appears in autumn.

H: 2m (6ft), **S**: 2m (6ft)
❄❄❄ ◊ ☼ ♈

Rosmarinus officinalis

This dense evergreen has strongly aromatic foliage and attractive blue flowers in spring and sometimes autumn. It will grow well in pots, is drought-tolerant, and responds well to trimming. It is a useful herb for cooking.

H: 1.5m (5ft), **S**: 1.5m (5ft)
❄❄ ◊ ☼

Salvia officinalis '*Purpurascens*'
Purple sage is a useful plant for the smaller garden: it is easy, quick-growing, and has aromatic, oval, soft, purple leaves. The plant forms ground-covering mounds, and in summer sends up flowering stems with small purple blooms.

H: 1m (3ft), **S**: 1m (3ft)
❋❋ ◊ ☼ ♔

Salvia x sylvestris '*Mainacht*'
Many salvias are first-rate plants for their summer flowers; this compact selection is useful in the smaller plot. Its early summer flowers are of an intense purplish-blue that is unusual for the time of year. They are carried in profusion in stiff upright spikes.

H: 1m (3ft), **S**: 50cm (20in)
❋❋ ◊ ☼ ♔

Stipa gigantea
The perennial giant oat, although large, is manageable in almost any garden. It forms a low hummock of long, narrow leaves, and in summer, produces tall stems bearing transparent golden flowerheads that shimmer in the breeze.

H: 2m (6ft), **S**: 1m (3ft)
❋❋❋ ◊ ◖ ☼ ♔

Trachycarpus wagnerianus
This is the perfect hardy palm for smaller plots, as it is slow-growing and compact. The plant forms a trunk gradually and is furnished with fan-shaped, dark, evergreen, deeply pleated leaves that give it a most refined appearance.

H: 2m (6ft) after 10 years, **S**: 2m (6ft)
❋❋❋ ◊ ◖ ☼ ☼

Verbena bonariensis
This "must-have" perennial is a useful plant even in small gardens because, although tall, it has a transparent quality, allowing views to planting behind. It is long-flowering, with heads of purple blooms appearing in summer and lasting into autumn.

H: 2m (6ft), **S**: 60cm (24in)
❋❋ ◊ ☼ ♔

Weigela '*Eva Rathke*'
These shrubs are grown for their spring and early summer blossom. This compact selection forms a dense shrub. Dark red flower buds appear in profusion in late spring and open to crimson, funnel-shaped flowers. Remove oldest stems after flowering.

H: 1.5m (5ft), **S**: 1.5m (5ft)
❋❋❋ ◊ ☼ ☼

Medium-sized plants for shade (Ac–De)

Acer shirasawanum 'Aureum'

This slow-growing, compact plant is striking, especially in late spring and early summer when its foliage is at its best. As the golden leaves expand, they resemble little oriental fans, seen to best effect in shade where they stand out from other planting.

H: 1.5m (5ft) after 10 years, **S**: 1m (3ft)

Anemanthele lessoniana

This grass is better known as *Stipa arundinacea*. It makes a neat clump of fairly broad, evergreen foliage, the leaves arching attractively. In late summer, tiny flowers are produced. In autumn, the clump develops russet tints, adding to its desirability.

H: 1.2m (4ft), **S**: 1.2m (4ft)

Anemone x hybrida 'Honorine Jobert'

There are few perennials to match this noble plant in late summer. Vigorous clumps of bold, divided foliage build steam through the summer until flowering stems appear, topped by sprays of single, white flowers.

H: 1.5m (5ft), **S**: 60cm (24in)

Aquilegia McKana Group

A cottage-garden favourite, this perennial is a good choice for its spring flowers in a wide range of different colours. The clumps of foliage develop in spring and are soon topped by distinctive flowers lasting for several weeks.

H: 1m (3ft), **S**: 50cm (20in)

Aruncus dioicus

This large, but easy-to-grow perennial is suited to moist sites. In spring, shoots soon form hummocks of leafy stems. By midsummer, plumes of tiny creamy-white flowers appear. They are held in handsome flowerheads and last for several weeks.

H: 2m (6ft), **S**: 1.2m (4ft)

Astilboides tabularis

A plant of great beauty, this species' main feature is its large, parasol-like leaves, each roughly circular, with the leaf stem attached to the centre. Soft green and delicate in early summer, they darken as the season progresses. White flowers appear in late summer.

H: 1.5m (5ft), **S**: 1m (3ft)

Aucuba japonica

This evergreen deserves recognition as one of the best hardy shrubs for year-round appeal. It will also withstand mistreatment. Its large oval leaves are spangled with golden spots. In spring, heads of red-purple flowers appear that develop into crimson berries.

H: 2.5m (8ft), **S**: 2.5m (8ft)
✽✽✽ ◊ ◊ ◖ ☼

Berberis darwinii

This spiny evergreen is one of the most spectacular spring-flowering shrubs and deserves a spot at the back of a border. The glossy foliage is an attractive foil to the clusters of bright orange flowers that cover the plant, followed later by blue berries.

H: 2m (6ft) after 10 years, **S**: 2m (6ft)
✽✽✽ ◊ ◖ ☼ ♈

Camellia japonica 'Bob's Tinsie'

This plant is a favourite, thanks to its unusual flowers and neat, compact habit. The glossy, oval, evergreen foliage is a good foil to the small, cup-shaped, red flowers that appear in abundance throughout spring.

H: 1.5m (5ft), **S**: 1m (3ft)
✽✽✽ ◊ ◖ ☼ ♈

Cornus sanguinea 'Winter Beauty'

This shrub is grown for the colour of its twigs. In summer, it is forgettable, but once the leaves turn butter-yellow in autumn, the show begins. The stems are bright orange-yellow, the younger shoots tinged red, making the plant look like a glowing flame.

H: 2m (6ft), **S**: 2m (6ft)
✽✽✽ ◖ ☼ ☼

Cotoneaster horizontalis

This shrub has much to recommend it. In spring, the soft green foliage is the attraction, followed by pink-white flowers in summer. In autumn, the leaves turn crimson before they fall; in winter, the stems are often peppered with red berries.

H: 2m (6ft), **S**: 2m (6ft)
✽✽✽ ◊ ◖ ☼ ☼ ♈

Desfontainia spinosa

At first glance, this plant resembles a compact holly with its small, dark, spine-edged leaves. In summer, it has a trick up its sleeve: long, tubular, pendent, red and yellow flowers appear, and are of great beauty, especially against the dark foliage.

H: 1m (3ft), **S**: 60cm (24in)
✽✽ ◖ ☼ ♈

Medium-sized plants for shade (Di–Le)

Dicentra spectabilis
The bleeding heart is a popular plant for light shade. Fleshy shoots emerge as winter ends and are easily damaged by late frosts. The soft foliage, which dies down in midsummer, is topped by arching sprays of pink and white flowers that last for several weeks.

H: 1m (3ft), **S**: 60cm (24in)
❄❄❄ ◯ ◑ ◐ 🏆

Digitalis purpurea
The foxglove is easy to grow, thrives in shade, and seeds freely. It is usually a biennial, which means it lives two years, building up a rosette of large oval leaves in the first, and producing its tall flower spike in the second. The flowers are usually purple or white.

H: 2m (6ft), **S**: 60cm (24in)
❄❄❄ ◑ ☼ ◐

Geranium x oxonianum *'Claridge Druce'*
This herbaceous plant is one of the toughest, and ideal for dry shade. It develops a mound of foliage that is often semi-evergreen, above which appear bright pink flowers from spring until late autumn.

H: 1.2m (4ft), **S**: 1m (3ft)
❄❄❄ ◯ ◑ ● ☼ ◐

Hedychium densiflorum
This hardy ginger makes a fine late-flowering perennial. In summer, it develops vigorous, fleshy shoots that grow quickly and display lush foliage. At the tips of each shoot appear spikes of scented, orange flowers that are produced well into autumn.

H: 1.2m (4ft), **S**: 2m (6ft)
❄❄ ◯ ◑ ☼ ◐

Helleborus argutifolius
This evergreen perennial is a useful plant, growing well in shade and filling gaps with its handsome serrated foliage, held on rather shrubby stems. In winter, bright green, open flowers appear. After flowering, stems wither and yellow and should be cut out.

H: 1m (3ft), **S**: 1m (3ft)
❄❄ ◯ ◑ ☼ ◐ 🏆

Hosta *'Jade Cascade'*
This huge, sturdy yet elegant hosta is well named. The long, pointed, rich green leaves, up to 30cm (12in) long, are strongly veined and held in a distinctive, downward-facing way on tall leaf stems. In early summer, tall spires of lilac blooms appear.

H: 1.2m (4ft), **S**: 1.1m (3½ft)
❄❄❄ ◑ ◐

Hosta sieboldiana

This large hosta has fine foliage. The leaves, which emerge from blue, tooth-like shoots in spring, are blue-grey at first, developing a green tinge as they age. Mature clumps make large mounds of puckered leaves 30cm (12in) long and as much across.

H: 1m (3ft), **S**: 1m (3ft)
✿✿✿ ◊ ☼

Hosta 'Sum and Substance'

A spectacular hosta cultivar that is one of the largest and easiest to grow of all, with huge golden-green leaves, especially bright as they first emerge in spring. In summer, tall spikes of lavender flowers appear. This hosta is also relatively slug-resistant.

H: 75cm (30in), **S**: 1.2m (4ft)
✿✿✿ ◊ ☼ ♈

Hydrangea macrophylla 'Lanarth White'

This hydrangea forms a rounded dome of growth. The flattened heads are composed of tiny blue or pink fertile flowers surrounded by pure white florets, and appear in late summer. The flowers show up best in shade.

H: 1m (3ft), **S**: 1m (3ft)
✿✿✿ ◊ ◊ ☼ ♈

Ilex crenata var. latifolia

This holly looks rather like box, but it is quicker growing. It responds well to trimming and can be kept as a low hedge. Other selections include *I. crenata* 'Golden Gem', which has glowing yellow foliage and makes a superb plant for shade.

H: up to 1.5m (5ft), **S**: 1.5m (5ft)
✿✿✿ ◊ ◊ ☼ ☼

Iris foetidissima

A UK native, this perennial is great for shade, even under trees and shrubs. The lance-shaped foliage remains in good condition in winter, and in spring, purple flowers appear. The orange seeds, which remain showy all winter, are the main talking point.

H: 1m (3ft), **S**: 60cm (24in)
✿✿✿ ◊ ◊ ☼ ♈

Leucothoe fontanesiana 'Rainbow'

A clump-forming evergreen shrub with an attractive, arching, fountain-shaped habit. The leaves are splashed and flecked with cream, pink, and orange. In summer, white, bell-shaped flowers hang from the stems.

H: 1.5m (5ft), **S**: 1.2m (4ft)
✿✿✿ ◊ ☼

Medium-sized plants for shade (Le–Vi)

Leycesteria formosa

An excellent shrub for a range of situations, including dry shade. In summer, clusters of pinky-purple flowers hang from arching stems amid lush oval leaves. By autumn, purple berries develop. The green stems are attractive in winter.

H: 1.5m (5ft), **S**: 1.2m (4ft)
❄❄❄ ◊ ◗ ☼ ◑ ♥

Ligularia dentata 'Desdemona'

This leafy perennial is a dramatic choice for moist sites. Clumps of large, rounded leaves flushed with purple are held on long stems, which appear from the ground in spring. These are followed by tall stems with orangy-yellow, daisy-like flowers.

H: 1.2m (4ft), **S**: 60cm (24in)
❄❄❄ ◊ ◗ ☼ ♥

Osmunda regalis

A large, deciduous fern, ideal for moist areas. In spring, croziers unwind from the ground and fresh, bright green fronds unfurl. Clumps provide an architectural element in summer; in autumn, they turn bright yellow.

H: 1.2m (4ft), **S**: 1m (3ft)
❄❄❄ ◊ ◗ ☼ ♥

Pieris 'Forest Flame'

This evergreen shrub is grown for its dramatic, bright red shoots and sprays of white, bell-shaped flowers. The flowers appear in early spring before the scarlet shoots. As the leaves mature, they fade to pink before turning green. It needs acidic soil.

H: 2.5m (8ft), **S**: 2m (6ft)
❄❄❄ ◊ ☼ ♥

Primula florindae

The largest and most spectacular of primulas, this perennial resembles a giant cowslip. Clumps of broad, soft green leaves 30cm (12in) long develop in spring, followed by tall flower stems that carry scented, bell-shaped flowers in yellow or orange.

H: 1.2m (4ft), **S**: 60cm (24in)
❄❄❄ ◊ ☼ ♥

Rhododendron 'Olive'

This evergreen rhododendron needs a sheltered position and acid soil to do well. The small, green, oval leaves serve as a good foil to the clusters of bright mauve-pink, funnel-shaped flowers up to 4cm (1½in) across. These are produced in late winter.

H: 1.5m (5ft), **S**: 1m (3ft)
❄❄❄ ◊ ☼

Rhododendron 'Persil'
This plant is a wonderful sight in late spring. Heads of large, scented, white flowers with a yellow flash in the centre appear at the same time as the soft, hairy leaves. The flowers last for several weeks, and show up well in shade. The plant needs acidic soil.

H: up to 2m (6ft), **S**: 2m (6ft)
❀❀❀ ◊ ☼ ☼ ♔

Ribes sanguineum 'Brocklebankii'
This compact flowering currant is most attractive in spring, the pink flowers appearing at the same time as the yellow leaves – to spectacular effect. This plant shows up well in shade and grows better out of sun because the leaves can scorch.

H: 1.5m (5ft), **S**: 1m (3ft)
❀❀❀ ◊ ☼

Sarcococca hookeriana var. digyna
Evergreen, compact, and winter flowering, this shade-loving plant is ideal for small gardens. The narrow leaves are shiny and the plant forms a dense, rounded mound. In winter, small, white tassels appear: these have a delicious, spicy scent.

H: 1m (3ft), **S**: 1m (3ft)
❀❀❀ ◊ ◊ ☼ ♔

Skimmia x confusa 'Kew Green'
With its glossy, pointed leaves, this skimmia cultivar is one of the most reliable. The large, conical, greenish-cream flowerheads, produced in early spring, have a delicious scent. This is a male plant; for berries, a female or hermaphrodite plant is required.

H: 1m (3ft), **S**: 1.5m (5ft)
❀❀❀ ◊ ☼ ♔

Viburnum davidii
This evergreen shrub, which forms a low mound, is a plant for all seasons. The oval leaves are attractively pleated and rich green. In summer, large heads of small, white flowers appear. Bright blue berries follow, provided male and female plants are grown.

H: 1m (3ft), **S**: 2m (6ft)
❀❀ ◊ ◊ ☼ ♔

Viburnum tinus 'Eve Price'
A compact and free-flowering evergreen plant that makes an ideal backdrop at the back of a border. It forms dense cover and has small, green, oval leaves. Heads of pink-tinged flowers are displayed through winter and spring.

H: 2m (6ft), **S**: 2m (6ft)
❀❀❀ ◊ ◊ ☼ ☼ ♔

Short plants for sun (Al–Di)

Allium schoenoprasum

Chives are not only useful in a herb garden – they are also an easy-to-grow choice for a flower garden and ideal as border edging. The narrow, blue-green leaves are especially attractive when topped by pinkish-mauve flowers that last several weeks.

H: 30cm (12in), **S**: 20cm (8in)
❀❀❀ ◊ ☼

Artemisia alba 'Canescens'

This useful front-of-border perennial, with its silver leaves, should be more widely grown. The lacy foliage is held on stems that tend to sprawl, covering the soil well. Cut plants to the ground in a cold winter, and new shoots will appear in spring.

H: 30cm (12in), **S**: 30cm (12in)
❀❀ ◊ ☼ ♈

Aster 'Coombe Fishacre'

In early autumn, few plants can compete with asters. This selection has a long flowering period and is well suited to smaller gardens. The blooms are daisy-like, pink with a darker eye, and appear in a multitude, lasting until the frosts.

H: 60cm (24in), **S**: 60cm (24in)
❀❀❀ ◊ ☼ ♈

Astrantia major

These beautiful perennials are becoming popular, thanks to the range now available. Clumps of leaves appear in spring and are topped by dainty flowers held on tall stems. The showy white or pink bracts resemble petals and encircle the true flowers.

H: 45cm (18in), **S**: 30cm (12in)
❀❀❀ ◊ ☼ ☼

Bergenia purpurascens

This perennial has beautiful foliage and flowers. It is more compact and has a longer season of interest than most bergenias, so it is better suited to small gardens. The glossy foliage develops rich purple tints in winter; in spring, pinkish-purple flowers appear.

H: 30cm (12in), **S**: 60cm (24in)
❀❀❀ ◊ ☼ ☼ ♈

Calluna vulgaris 'Silver Knight'

For silver foliage, few heathers create a better effect than this shrubby, evergreen plant. When mature, it produces a wonderful wispy silver cloud of dense, quite upright, but ground-covering, growth. Although easy to grow, it must have acid soil.

H: 30cm (12in), **S**: 60cm (24in)
❀❀❀ ◊ ◊ ☼

Campanula glomerata
One of the simplest campanulas to grow, this low, spreading perennial makes good summer ground cover, and self-seeds freely. From early summer until autumn, heads of bell-shaped blue or white flowers appear on short stems.

H: 30cm (12in), **S**: 1m (3ft)
✳✳✳ ◊ ◊ ☼ ☼

Catananche caerulea
This sun-loving perennial is grown for its lavender-blue flowers, which look rather like pale cornflowers, produced in summer and autumn. The blooms are held on a wiry stalk above clumps of silvery foliage. They combine well with other pale-coloured plants.

H: 60cm (24in), **S**: 30cm (12in)
✳✳ ◊ ☼

Ceratostigma plumbaginoides
Easy to grow, this low shrub flowers when most other plants have finished. It spreads at the root and, under ideal conditions, forms a large clump. The rich blue flowers are held in clusters above the leaves, which turn red before falling.

H: 30cm (12in), **S**: 60cm (24in)
✳✳ ◊ ☼ ♈

Cerinthe major
Growing swiftly from seed, this annual develops into a low bush, covered in blue-silver leaves. Long-lasting, purple, bell-shaped flowers appear in late spring, giving an attractive, almost iridescent appearance. It self-seeds freely.

H: 45cm (18in), **S**: 30cm (12in)
✳✳✳ ◊ ☼

Convolvulus cneorum
This evergreen, low-growing shrub is grown both for its soft, bright silver foliage and the multitude of white, cup-shaped flowers that appear in summer. Each flower lasts little more than a day but the bush is covered in blooms for weeks.

H: 50cm (20in), **S**: 1m (3ft)
✳✳ ◊ ☼ ♈

Diascia barberae 'Blackthorn Apricot'
Often grown as an annual, this plant is perennial in the right position. Although cut to the ground in winter, new stems appear in spring to make a small sprawling clump. The stems bear peach-coloured flowers all summer.

H: 30cm (12in), **S**: 30cm (12in)
✳✳ ◊ ☼ ♈

Short plants for sun (Er–Ge)

Erica carnea 'Foxhollow'

There are many winter-flowering heathers but this is a favourite, bearing small, pale pink, bell-shaped flowers throughout the coldest weather. The needle-like, pale green leaves become tinged with red in winter. A good low-growing plant.

H: 20cm (8in), **S**: 60cm (24in)

✻✻✻ ◊ ◑ ☼ ♈

Erigeron karvinskianus

The little Mexican daisy is a welcome plant in many gardens, often growing in gaps in paving or out of dry stone walls – anywhere hot and dry. The small pink-tinged white daisy flowers appear from early summer to winter on low sprawling plants.

H: 20cm (8in), **S**: 60cm (24in)

✻✻ ◊ ☼ ♈

Erysimum 'Bowles' Mauve'

This is a superb plant for injecting colour into cottage garden-style planting in spring and summer. It forms an evergreen, shrubby plant with grey-green leaves. In spring, the flowering stems are soon covered with purple flowers.

H: 60cm (24in), **S**: 60cm (24in)

✻✻ ◊ ☼ ♈

Euphorbia cyparissias 'Fens Ruby'

This low-growing perennial is a useful, if somewhat invasive plant, grown for its foliage and spring flowers. In spring, purplish-green shoots appear, producing delicate foliage. As the season progresses, small, lime-green flowers develop.

H: 30cm (12in), **S**: 2m (6ft)

✻✻✻ ◊ ◑ ☼

Euphorbia rigida

This sprawling plant is superb in a sunny rockery. Fleshy stems arise from a central crown, then grow along the ground in an almost snake-like fashion, holding narrow, triangular blue-silver leaves. Lime-green flowers appear in early summer.

H: 20cm (8in), **S**: 60cm (24in)

✻✻ ◊ ☼

Francoa sonchifolia

In a sunny, warm area, this perennial makes good ground cover. The fleshy leaves grow from a creeping stem, which in mid- to late summer sends up tall stems, well above the foliage, of pale pink flowers spotted with darker pink.

H: 60cm (24in), **S**: 60cm (24in)

✻✻ ◊ ☼ ☼

Fuchsia *'Genii'*

This compact, hardy fuchsia is a reliable cultivar. It produces masses of pendent purple and red flowers in late summer and autumn, until the first frosts. The blooms are held against bright yellow leaves, adding to the plant's impact.

H: 60cm (24in), **S**: 60cm (24in)
❄❄ ◊ ☼ ◑ ♔

Gaura lindheimeri

A delicate-looking perennial for the front of a sunny border that produces wands of open, white flowers held on slim stems from midsummer until mid-autumn. Hard frosts will kill the top growth but fresh shoots appear in spring if protected in winter.

H: up to 1m (36in), **S**: 1m (3ft)
❄❄ ◊ ☼ ◑ ♔

Geranium *'Ann Folkard'*

This hardy geranium is appealing for both flowers and foliage. The leaves are hand-shaped and bright gold in colour, especially when young; they become greener as they age. Large, open, bright magenta flowers with dark centres are produced all summer.

H: 60cm (24in), **S**: 1m (3ft)
❄❄❄ ◊ ☼ ◑ ♔

Geranium *Rozanne* ('*Gerwat*')

One of the finest of all hardy geraniums, this selection has trailing, non-rooting stems that cover the ground from late spring, producing masses of large, open bright blue flowers from early summer well into autumn. Cut back stems in winter.

H: 45cm (18in), **S**: 60cm (24in)
❄❄❄ ◊ ☼ ◑

Geum coccineum

This clump-forming perennial is a fine summer-flowering plant. It forms a rosette of toothed green leaves, and attractive, open, saucer-shaped, orange-red flowers with yellow stamens for several weeks. Plants like sun but not overly dry soil.

H: 50cm (20in), **S**: 30cm (12in)
❄❄❄ ◊ ◊ ☼ ◑

Geum rivale

A European native, the little water avens is attractive for wet areas in perhaps wilder patches of the garden. This perennial forms clumps of leaves, and over several weeks in early summer produces dusky pink and red bell-shaped flowers.

H: 50cm (20in), **S**: 30cm (12in)
❄❄❄ ◊ ◊ ☼

Short plants for sun (Ha–Pe)

Hakonechloa macra 'Aureola'

This ornamental grass is a fine garden plant. It forms a low clump of gold and green striped foliage. The plant spreads slowly from slender rhizomes and will grow in a range of situations, including sun, as long as the soil is moist.

H: 30cm (12in), **S**: 40cm (16in)
❀❀❀ ◊ ◑ ☼ ◐ ☀ ☍ ♈

Helianthemum 'Rhodanthe Carneum' ('Wisley Pink')

This low-growing plant is ideal for sunny rockeries. Plants are evergreen with small, oval, silvery foliage. In early summer, silver-pink flowers with a soft yellow eye appear. They last a day, but are produced in profusion.

H: 30cm (12in), **S**: 50cm (20in)
❀❀❀ ◊ ☼ ♈

Hemerocallis 'Golden Chimes'

A dainty day lily, ideal for the small garden because it is compact and free-flowering. In summer, flowering stems appear from clumps of narrow, arching leaves. The bright yellow, open, trumpet-shaped flowers have brownish-red reverses.

H: up to 1m (3ft), **S**: 50cm (20in)
❀❀❀ ◊ ☼ ◐ ♈ ♈

Hypericum olympicum

An ideal plant for open, sunny positions, this low-growing shrub is a fine sight in summer. The small leaves are grey-green and a good foil to the open, starry, golden-yellow flowers produced in clusters at the ends of the stems.

H: 30cm (12in), **S**: 50cm (20in)
❀❀❀ ◊ ☼ ♈

Iris unguicularis

Few herbaceous plants are of interest in winter but this evergreen iris is a stellular performer. For much of the year it is unremarkable, but in mild spells during winter, delicate lavender-mauve flowers with yellow markings open, lasting several days.

H: 30cm (12in), **S**: 60cm (24in)
❀❀❀ ◊ ☼ ♈

Lychnis flos-cuculi

The ragged robin is a European native. It is a short-lived perennial that sends up tall flowering stems in early summer. The flowers are open, starry, usually pale pink, sometimes white, with long narrow petals. Plants grow well in damp shade.

H: 75cm (30in), **S**: 30cm (12in)
❀❀❀ ◊ ◑ ☼ ◐

Narcissus 'Jetfire'

There are many narcissi to choose from but this selection, with its elegant and brightly coloured early spring blooms, is a favourite. The flower petals are rich gold and reflexed, while the trumpet is a contrasting reddish-orange.

H: 22cm (9in), **S**: 10cm (4in)
❋❋❋ ◊ ☀ ☼ ☀ ♈

Nepeta x faassenii

Useful and easy, catmint is a clump-forming plant with spreading stems and blue-green, soft, aromatic foliage that is attractive to cats. In summer, sprays of blue flowers appear. If the plant is cut back after flowering, it will produce a second crop.

H: 50cm (20in), **S**: 50cm (20in)
❋❋❋ ◊ ☀ ♈

Oenothera speciosa

Low-growing and sun-loving, this plant spreads freely at the root, especially in light soil, producing short, upright stems. The large, cup-shaped, pink flowers open from pointed buds and are short-lived, but appear in great profusion throughout summer.

H: 30cm (12in), **S**: 50cm (20in)
❋❋❋ ◊ ☀

Osteospermum 'Sunny Serena'

A tender perennial, grown for its dazzling daisy flowers in summer and well into autumn, this plant is well suited to container cultivation or filling gaps in sunny beds and borders. Remove blooms as they fade and apply feed regularly if in a pot.

H: 60cm (24in), **S**: 30cm (12in)
❋ ◊ ☀

Penstemon 'Alice Hindley'

With its shimmering, pale mauve-violet flowers carried in upright flowerheads, this is one of the most desirable penstemons. Oval leaves are carried on woody stems that should not be cut back until spring when new shoots arise from the base of the plant.

H: 75cm (30in), **S**: 50cm (20in)
❋❋ ◊ ☀ ♈

Penstemon 'Andenken an Friedrich Hahn'

A most popular penstemon, this plant is better known as *P.* 'Garnet'. Loose but upright flowerheads of rich red, tubular blooms appear throughout summer and well into autumn, until the first frosts.

H: 75cm (30in), **S**: 60cm (24in)
❋❋ ◊ ☀ ♈

Short plants for sun (Pe–Za)

Persicaria affinis 'Superba'

For ground cover, there are few plants to match this perennial, particularly in late summer and autumn when the the blooms open pale pink and age to crimson, giving a fine two-tone look on the same plant. Rust-brown leaves carpet the ground in winter.

H: 30cm (12in), **S**: 60cm (24in)
❋❋❋ ◊ ◊ ☼ ☼ ☼ ♈ ♈

Phlox 'Chattahoochee'

A low-growing perennial that is ideal for the front of a border or a rockery. In early summer, flowers are carried in clusters. They are a delightful rich lilac colour with a central reddish-purple eye, and are produced in profusion.

H: 30cm (12in), **S**: 60cm (24in)
❋❋❋ ◊ ☼ ☼ ☼

Pittosporum tenuifolium 'Tom Thumb'

This evergreen makes a great addition to the smaller garden, with its compact form and mahogany coloured foliage. The leaves are particularly attractive in spring as green new growth emerges, giving the plant a two-tone effect.

H: up to 1m (3ft), **S**: 60cm (24in)
❋❋ ◊ ☼ ♈

Pulsatilla vulgaris

The pasque flower is one of the most beautiful spring flowers. The fern-like foliage forms a small clump, while its star-shaped flowers are usually rich purple, but can be pink, red, or white, and have a boss of golden stamens. The plant prefers a chalky soil.

H: 30cm (12in), **S**: 20cm (8in)
❋❋❋ ◊ ☼ ♈

Rudbeckia fulgida *var.* sullivantii 'Goldsturm'

Perennials that flower in autumn are valuable and this plant is also compact. Its daisy-like flowers, with narrow, golden petals and a black central cone, open atop stout stems, which should be cut to the ground after flowering.

H: 60cm (24in), **S**: 60cm (24in)
❋❋❋ ◊ ◊ ☼ ♈

Sedum 'Herbstfreude'

With its succulent grey-green stems and foliage, this plant is well adapted to withstand hot sun and drought. In late summer, flat heads of rust-red flowers open, lasting for several weeks; the dry flowerheads remain attractive into winter.

H: 60cm (24in), **S**: 1m (3ft)
❋❋❋ ◊ ☼ ♈

Sisyrinchium striatum '*Aunt May*'
This choice plant earns its keep. All year, the rapier-like foliage, striped lengthways with cream and grey-green, provides striking contrast to more rounded shapes. In early summer, spikes of primrose-yellow flowers open in succession.

H: 60cm (24in), **S**: 30cm (12in)
❀❀ ◊ ☼ ♈

Stachys byzantina '*Big Ears*'
This selection of the common lambs' ears has large, oval leaves, which are covered with silvery-white "wool". The low-growing plant is particularly attractive at the front of a pale-coloured border. In summer, erect spikes of mauve flowers appear.

H: 60cm (24in), **S**: 1m (3ft)
❀❀❀ ◊ ☼

Stipa tenuissima
This perennial grass is a good choice for the garden as it is beautiful for much of the year. In spring, the bright green growth is attractive, but in summer, the flowerheads give clumps a fluffy appearance, and as the seeds form, plants become straw-coloured.

H: 60cm (24in), **S**: 30cm (12in)
❀❀ ◊ ☼ ♈

**Veronica gentianoides
'*Tissington White*'**
A good plant for early summer, this low-growing perennial carpets the ground with its shiny oval leaves. Numerous spikes of grey-white flowers arise in late spring and remain attractive for several weeks.

H: 60cm (24in), **S**: 60cm (24in)
❀❀❀ ◊ ◑ ☼ ♈

Vinca difformis
Periwinkles are popular ground-covering plants, but this species is more refined than many. The flowers are the plant's star turn. They are produced through much of winter and spring and are pale blue to nearly white and propeller-shaped.

H: 60cm (24in), **S**: 1.2m (4ft)
❀❀ ◊ ☼ ◑ ♈

Zauschneria californica
Spectacular in flower, this plant needs a hot situation to grow well, but is an excellent choice for a sunny corner. It forms a low plant with small grey-green leaves. In late summer, sprays of vibrant, orange-red flowers appear, each bloom shaped like a small fuchsia.

H: 60cm (24in), **S**: 60cm (24in)
❀❀ ◊ ☼

Short plants for shade (Al–He)

Alchemilla mollis
Commonly known as lady's mantle, this perennial thrives in the shade. The soft green leaves form a mound of growth, and have a charming way of catching water droplets. In summer, heads of lime-green small flowers appear.

H: 30cm (12in), **S**: 60cm (24in)
❋❋❋ ◊ ☀ ♛

Arum italicum *subsp*. italicum 'Marmoratum'
This perennial is grown for its winter foliage. Leathery leaves, richly veined in silver-white, appear in late autumn. The green flowers in summer are uneventful, but later displays of red berries (poisonous) are attractive.

H: 60cm (24in), **S**: 30cm (12in)
❋❋❋ ◊ ◊ ☀ ♛

Brunnera macrophylla 'Dawson's White'
This compact perennial needs a cool, moist position. The hairy, heart-shaped leaves, margined with white, are particularly attractive with the sprays of blue flowers that are carried on stems above the foliage.

H: 30cm (12in), **S**: 30cm (12in)
❋❋❋ ◊ ◊ ☀

Carex elata 'Aurea'
With vibrant fountains of rich, golden, grassy foliage, this clump-forming deciduous perennial is a desirable plant for moist, even wet, soil in shade. Here, it shines out from darker plants, especially in spring when the leaves are young.

H: 70cm (28in), **S**: 45cm (18in)
❋❋❋ ◊ ◊ ☀ ♛

Cornus canadensis
A seldom-seen ground-cover plant that spreads by rhizomes in acidic soil. The leaves are held around short stems, and showy white flowerheads are borne in early summer. Each has four "petals" that are actually bracts, and may be followed by red berries.

H: 20cm (8in), **S**: 1m (3ft)
❋❋❋ ◊ ☀ ♛

Corydalis flexuosa
This dainty perennial is easy to grow in a cool corner. It comes into growth early, fleshy shoots producing fern-like leaves. The electric-blue flowers are held in clusters and look rather like shoals of little fish. After flowering, plants often die down quickly.

H: 20cm (8in), **S**: 60cm (24in)
❋❋❋ ◊ ☀ ♛

Cyclamen hederifolium

This is an essential plant for its autumn flower displays. The plant grows from a corm just below the surface of the soil, sending up masses of pink or white flowers, followed by attractive leaves that are marked with silver or darker green.

H: 10cm (4in), **S**: 20cm (8in)
✺✺✺ ◊ ◊ ☼ ♆

Daphne laureola *subsp.* philippi

This upright bushy evergreen is slow-growing and suited to the smaller plot. The leaves are shiny and clustered towards the tops of the stems, from where, in late winter, strongly perfumed, green bell-shaped flowers appear, followed by black berries.

H: 60cm (24in), **S**: 1m (3ft)
✺✺✺ ◊ ◊ ☼

Epimedium *x* versicolor

These easy-to-grow, clump-forming perennials are good for shaded spots under shrubs. The dainty, divided foliage is attractive, especially in spring, and is often bronze-tinged. Clusters of yellow, orange, or pink flowers appear at the same time.

H: 20cm (8in), **S**: 30cm (12in)
✺✺✺ ◊ ◊ ☼ ♆

Galanthus nivalis

The first flowers of the common snowdrop are a sign to gardeners that spring is on the way. These plants grow well in shade and will quickly bulk up to form large clumps, which need to be split regularly to keep them flowering.

H: 10cm (4in), **S**: 20cm (8in)
✺✺✺ ◊ ◊ ☼ ♆

Geranium macrorrhizum

This is one of the lower-growing hardy geraniums, good for planting under larger shrubs and forming dense ground cover with its soft aromatic foliage. In spring, short stems produce clusters of pink, mauve, or white flowers over several weeks.

H: 30cm (12in), **S**: 60cm (24in)
✺✺✺ ◊ ◊ ☼

Helleborus *x* hybridus

Also known as Lenten roses, these perennials are very popular spring plants. In late winter, new shoots emerge; the nodding flowers appear first, followed by the leaves. The flowers come in many colours except blue, and they last for weeks.

H: 50cm (20in), **S**: 30cm (12in)
✺✺✺ ◊ ◊ ☼

Short plants for shade (He–Uv)

Heuchera 'Plum Pudding'
This foliage plant makes an attractive addition to a shady border. The rounded, evergreen, wavy-edged leaves are purple-red with silver markings that give the plant a metallic shimmer. In summer, spires of flowers are held above the foliage.

H: 60cm (24in), **S**: 30cm (12in)
❀❀❀ ○ ◐ ☀ ☼

Lysimachia nummularia 'Aurea'
This perennial's brightly coloured foliage means it can be used in the garden to dramatic effect. The golden, oval leaves are held on stems that grow flat on the ground, forming a dense mat. Yellow, cup-shaped flowers appear in summer.

H: 3cm (1¼in), **S**: 1m (3ft)
❀❀❀ ○ ◐ ◑ ● ☼ ☼ ☼ ♔

Meconopsis cambrica
The delightful Welsh poppy is a welcome plant in many gardens; its fresh foliage and flowers make a wonderful show in shaded positions. The flowers, carried on slender stems above the leaves, appear in shades of yellow or orange.

H: 50cm (20in), **S**: 30cm (12in)
❀❀❀ ○ ◐ ☼ ☼ ♔

Omphalodes cappadocica 'Cherry Ingram'
This little perennial is a delight in spring. Its small leaves form a compact clump that starts early into growth. Starry, mauve-blue flowers are carried in small spires and are beautiful for several weeks.

H: 20cm (8in), **S**: 30cm (12in)
❀❀❀ ○ ◐ ☼ ☼ ♔

Ophiopogon planiscapus 'Nigrescens'
A useful perennial that can be combined with many other plants. It is clump-forming and evergreen with almost black, grass-like foliage. In summer, small, mauve flowers appear, followed by black berries.

H: 15cm (6in), **S**: 20cm (8in)
❀❀❀ ○ ◐ ☼ ♔

Pachysandra terminalis
This evergreen, ground-covering plant is one of few that will grow in dry shade under shrubs and trees. Its toothed leaves form a mat of growth that prevents weeds; the plant spreads via underground runners. In summer, white flowers appear.

H: 20cm (8in), **S**: 60cm (24in)
❀❀❀ ○ ◐ ☼

Primula pulverulenta

This perennial must have moist, rich soil to thrive. The leaves emerge in spring before the flowerheads. The stout stems, which are covered in a chalky white coating, are striking and contrast well with the rounded heads of small, reddish-purple blooms.

H: 60cm (24in), **S**: 30cm (12in)
❊❊❊ ◗ ◖ ☼ ♈

Primula vulgaris

The common primrose is a worthy garden plant and will grow in shady borders under trees and shrubs, in cool rockeries, or naturalized in rough grass. In early spring, a succession of yellow, or sometimes white, or even pink, flowers open over many weeks.

H: 15cm (6in), **S**: 20cm (8in)
❊❊❊ ◗ ☼ ♈

Pulmonaria 'Sissinghurst White'

With attractive, bell-shaped flowers produced over many weeks in spring, and silver-green foliage, these perennials are excellent garden plants. This dependable selection has white flowers that show up well in shade.

H: 20cm (8in), **S**: 60cm (24in)
❊❊❊ ◗ ☼ ♈

Saxifraga fortunei

This perennial is remarkable for its late-flowering habit, although some selections bloom during summer. It is a clump-forming plant with handsome, glossy, hand-shaped leaves. Showy flowerheads of white flowers appear before the frosts.

H: 50cm (20in), **S**: 30cm (12in)
❊❊❊ ◗ ◖ ☼

Tiarella cordifolia

A good ground-cover plant, this perennial spreads from runners, colonizing small areas. The hand-shaped leaves are soft and tinted purple. Small, white, pink-tinged flowers are held in short spires during spring.

H: 20cm (8in), **S**: 60cm (24in)
❊❊❊ ◗ ◖ ☼ ♈

Uvularia grandiflora

A most elegant perennial that bears flowers in mid-spring. Tall, slender stems with oval leaves arise, from which dangle bell-shaped, yellow flowers with long twisted petals. It is not an easy plant and likes a cool moist soil with added organic matter.

H: 60cm (24in), **S**: 30cm (12in)
❊❊❊ ◗ ◖ ☼ ♈

Index

Index

Acknowledgements

The publisher would like to thank the following for their kind permission to reproduce their photographs:

(Key: a-above; b-below/bottom; c-centre; l-left; r-right; t-top)

2–3: DK Images: Steve Wooster/RHS Chelsea Flower Show 2001. **6–7:** DK Images: Steve Wooster/RHS Chelsea Flower Show 2001/Norwood Hall, The Artist's Garden. **8:** Harpur Garden Library: Marcus Harpur/ Design: Dr Mary Giblin, Essex (t). Andrew Lawson: Designer: Anthony Noel (b). **9:** The Garden Collection: Liz Eddison (b). John Glover: Ladywood, Hampshire (t). **10:** The Garden Collection: Liz Eddison/Tatton Park Flower Show 2002/Designer: Andrew Walker. **11:** Marianne Majerus Photography: RHS Rosemoor (t), S & O Mathews Photography: The Lawrences' Garden, Hunterville, NZ (c), Leigh Clapp: (b). **12:** DK Images: Sarah Cuttle/RHS Chelsea Flower Show 2005/4Head Garden/ Designer: Marney Hall (tr), Mark Winwood/Hampton Court Flower Show 2005/Designer: Susan Slater (br). **14:** Marianne Majerus Photography/ Designer: Pat Wallace (t), Designer: Ann Frith (b). **15:** Marianne Majerus Photography/ Designer: George Carter (t), The Garden Collection: Jonathan Buckley/ Designer: Helen Yemm (b). **16:** Derek St Romaine/ RHS Chelsea Flower Show 2000/Designer: Lindsay Knight (t), The Garden Collection: Liz Eddison/Hampton Court Flower Show 2005/Designer: Daryl Gannon (b). **17:** The Garden Collection: Liz Eddison/Whichford Pottery (l); Liz Eddison/Hampton Court Flower Show 2002/Designer Maureen Busby (r). **18:** Andrew Lawson: (t) (c) (b). **19:** The Garden Collection: Jonathan Buckley/ Designer: Helen Yemm. **20:** The Garden Collection: Derek Harris. **21:** Leigh Clapp: St Michael's House (t). Andrew Lawson: (b). **22:** The Garden Collection: Liz Eddison/Hampton Court Flower Show 2001/Designer: Cherry Burton (t). **23:** Leigh Clapp: Green Lane Farm. **24:** Andrew Lawson. **25:** The Garden Collection: Jonathan Buckley/Designer: Mark Brown (t); Jonathan Buckley (b). **26:** Marianne Majerus Photography: Designer: Kathleen Beddington (t). **27:** The Garden Collection: Liz Eddison (tl), Andrew Lawson (r): Waterperry Gardens, Oxon (bl). **30:** John Glover: Ladywood, Hants (t). **32:** Derek St Romaine/ Mr & Mrs Bates, Surrey (t). Nicola Stocken Tomkins: Berrylands Road, Surrey (b). **33:** Marianne Majerus Photography/ Designer: Julie Toll (t), Leigh Clapp (b). **34:** Leigh Clapp: Copse Lodge (l). Nicola Stocken Tomkins: Longer End Cottage, Normandy, Surrey (c), Nicola Browne/ Designer: Jinny Blom (r). **35:** Leigh Clapp: Merriments Nursery (l). Andrew Lawson: RHS Chelsea Flower Show 1999/Selsdon & District Horticultural Society (c). Nicola Stocken Tomkins: Hampton Court Flower Show 2004/Designer: S Eberle (r). **37:** Marianne Majerus Photography: Manor Farm, Keisby, Lincs. (br). **42:** crocus.co.uk (bl). **46:** Andrew Lawson. **50:** Forest Garden (br). **71:** DK Images: Mark Winwood/ Capel Manor College/Designer: Irma Ansell: The Mediterranean Garden. **72–3:** Thompson & Morgan. **75:** DK Images: Mark Winwood/Capel Manor College/Designer: Elizabeth Ramsden: Modern Front Garden. **77:** DK Images: Mark Winwood/Hampton Court Flower Show 2005/Designer: Susan Slater: 'Pushing the Edge of the Square'. **78:** Marianne Majerus/Designers: Nori and Sandra Pope, Hadspen (bl). **79:** Marianne Majerus Photography/ Designers: Nori and Sandra Pope, Hadspen. **81:** DK Images: Mark Winwood/Hampton Court Flower Show 2005: Designed by Guildford College: 'Journey of the Senses'. **83:** DK Images: Mark Winwood/Capel Manor College/Designer: Sascha Dutton-Forshaw: 'Victorian Front Garden. **84–85:** DK Images: Mark Winwood/Capel Manor College/ Designer: Irma Ansell: The Mediterranean Garden. **87:** Modeste Herwig. **88:** Leigh Clapp/ Designers: Acres Wild (bl). **89:** Leigh Clapp/Designers: Acres Wild. **90:** S & O Mathews Photography: RHS Rosemoor (bl) (br). **91:** S & O Mathews Photography: RHS Rosemoor. **99:** John Glover. **118:** Holt Studios International: Michael Mayer/FLPA (bl). **119:** RHS, Tim Sandall (bc), Holt Studios International: Nigel Cattlin/FLPA (cr). **124:** crocus.co.uk (bl), **125:** crocus. co.uk (bc). **127:** crocus.co.uk (bc). **133:** crocus.co.uk (tr). **136:** Garden World Images: (bl). **148:** Garden World Images: (bl) (br)

All other images © Dorling Kindersley For further information see: www.dkimages.com

Dorling Kindersley would also like to thank the following:
Editors for Airedale Publishing: Helen Ridge, Fiona Wild, Mandy Lebentz
Designers for Airedale Publishing: Elly King, Murdo Culver
Index: Michèle Clarke

Gardening Which? (www.which.co.uk) and Capel Manor College (www.capel. ac.uk) for photography locations.